GREAT MYSTERIES

Unicorns

OPPOSING VIEWPOINTS®

Look for these and other exciting *Great Mysteries: Opposing Viewpoints* books:

Amelia Earhart *by Jane Leder*
Anastasia, Czarina or Fake?
    by Leslie McGuire
Animal Communication *by Jacci Cole*
The Assassination of President Kennedy
    by Jeffrey Waggoner
Atlantis *by Wendy Stein*
The Beginning of Language
    by Clarice Swisher
The Bermuda Triangle *by Norma Gaffron*
Bigfoot *by Norma Gaffron*
Dinosaurs *by Peter & Connie Roop*
The Discovery of America
    by Renardo Barden
ESP *by Michael Arvey*
The Loch Ness Monster *by Robert San Souci*
Noah's Ark *by Patricia Kite*
Pearl Harbor *by Deborah Bachrach*
Poltergeists *by Peter & Connie Roop*
Pyramids *by Barbara Mitchell*
Reincarnation *by Michael Arvey*
The Shroud of Turin *by Daniel C. Scavone*
The Solar System *by Peter & Connie Roop*
Stonehenge *by Peter & Connie Roop*
The Trojan War *by Gail Stewart*
UFOs *by Michael Arveyl*
Unicorns *by Norma Gaffron*
Witches *by Bryna Stevens*

GREAT MYSTERIES

Unicorns

OPPOSING VIEWPOINTS®

by Norma Gaffron

Greenhaven Press, Inc.   P.O. Box 289009, San Diego, California 92128-9009

Library of Congress Cataloging-in-Publication Data

Gaffron, Norma, 1931-
  Unicorns.

  (Great mysteries : opposing viewpoints)
  Bibliography: p.
  Includes index.
  Summary: Examines scientific and legendary sources to explore the existence of unicorns.
  1. Unicorns—Juvenile literature. [1. Unicorns]
I. Title. II. Series: Great mysteries (Saint Paul, Minn.)
GR830.U6G34 1989   398´.469   89-11660
ISBN 0-89908-063-4

*Dedicated to everyone who
believes in possibilities*

N.B.G.

*"Far on the edge of the world and
    beyond the banks of the Ganges,
Savage and lone, is a place in the realm
    of the King of the Hindus . . .
Where there is born a beast as large as
    a stag in stature,
Dark on the back, solid-hoofed, very
    fierce, and shaped like a bullock.
Mighty and black is the horn that springs
    from the animal's forehead. . . ."*

*From a poem written by Natalis Comes in
about the middle of the sixteenth century*

Contents

Introduction   9

One   A Special Creature   10

Two   Eastern Origins   20

Three   Rumor or Reality?   36

Four   The Spiritual Unicorn   42

Five   Medieval Times   54

Six   Science and the Unicorn   84

Epilogue Where Are the Unicorns Now?   102

Appendix The Unicorn Today   105

         For Further Exploration   107

         Additional Bibliography   108

         Index   109

         Picture Credits   111

         About the Author   112

Introduction

This book is written for the curious—those who want to explore the mysteries that are everywhere. To be human is to be constantly surrounded by wonderment. How do birds fly? Are ghosts real? Can animals and people communicate? Was King Arthur a real person or a myth? Why did Amelia Earhart disappear? Did history really happen the way we think it did? Where did the world come from? Where is it going?

Great Mysteries: Opposing Viewpoints books are intended to offer the reader an opportunity to explore some of the many mysteries that both trouble and intrigue us. For the span of each book, we want the reader to feel that he or she is a scientist investigating the extinction of the dinosaurs, an archaeologist searching for clues to the origin of the great Egyptian pyramids, a psychic detective testing the existence of ESP.

One thing all mysteries have in common is that there is no ready answer. Often there are *many* answers but none on which even the majority of authorities agrees. *Great Mysteries: Opposing Viewpoints* books introduce the intriguing views of the experts, allowing the reader to participate in their explorations, their theories, and their disagreements as they try to explain the mysteries of our world.

But most readers won't want to stop here. These *Great Mysteries: Opposing Viewpoints* aim to stimulate the reader's curiosity. Although truth is often impossible to discover, the search is fascinating. It is up to the reader to examine the evidence, to decide whether the answer is there—or to explore further.

"Penetrating so many secrets, we cease to believe in the unknowable. But there it sits nevertheless, calmly licking its chops."

H.L. Mencken, American essayist

One

A Special Creature

Genghis Khan was thirteen years old when he succeeded his father as a tribal chief of Mongolia, a country in eastern Asia. The year was 1180, and the tribe was unruly. But the boy, young as he was, was determined to become a strong leader. Eventually he brought his subjects under control, and then with the flush of victory on his brow, he looked for other tribes to conquer. By the time he was thirty-nine years old, Genghis Khan was the master of all Mongolia.

But for him this was not enough. He became restless. So when the emperor of China threatened the Mongols, demanding money from them, the khan was only too eager to again take on the role of warrior. With his army, he scaled the Great Wall and invaded northern China in 1215. After a series of bloody campaigns he took the frontier city of Chung-tu, now known as Beijing, or Peking. Mongolia would pay no tribute to foreign rulers.

By now Genghis Khan was possessed with the fever of conquest. Within three years he was on the move again. The area of China that is now Korea fell to the Mongol armies. Still the mighty military leader was not satisfied. He headed west. The countries now known as Iraq and Iran were brought under Mongol rule. Part of the Soviet Union succumbed next. By 1222, the khan's empire reached from the China Sea on the east to the Dnieper River in western Russia.

Above: Genghis Khan, fabled Mongol leader, is said to have changed his plans because of a unicorn.

On the south it was bounded by the Persian Gulf. On the north it extended to the Arctic Ocean. It seemed that nothing could stop Genghis Khan.

But something did.

Odell Shepard, in his book *The Lore of the Unicorn*, tells what happened:

The conqueror Genghis Khan set out with a great host to invade India. His army had marched for many days and had climbed through many mountain passes, but just when he reached the crest of the divide and looked down over the country he intended to subjugate, there came running toward him a beast with a single horn which bent its knee three times before him in token of reverence. And then, while all the host stood wondering, the Conqueror paused in his march and pondered. At last he said, as we are told in the vivid narrative of Ssanang Ssetsen: "This middle kingdom of India before us is the place, men say,

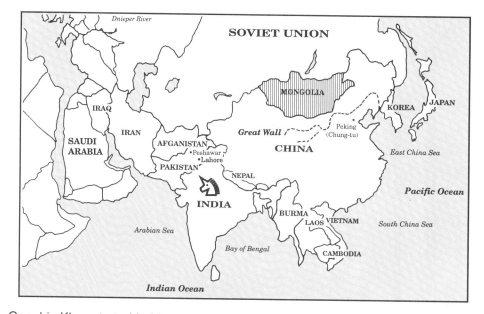

Genghis Khan started in Mongolia, but soon moved on to conquer much of Asia. (On this map, the countries are marked as we know them today.)

in which the sublime Buddha and the Bodhisatwas and many powerful princes of old time were born. What may it mean that this speechless wild animal bows before me like a man? Is it that the spirit of my father would send me a warning out of heaven?'' With these words he turned his army about and marched back again into his own land.

India had been saved by a unicorn.

The unicorn knelt before Genghis Khan, surely an omen of great importance. In this painting, the unicorn kneels before Procris, a character from Greek mythology.

"We may never know precisely when or where or how the legend of the unicorn began. It pervades recorded time and may be dimly visible even in the clouds that hover just above history's sunrise."

Odell Shepard, *The Lore of the Unicorn*

"It could have happened this way: thousands of years ago some Persian hunter saw an ibex in profile against the open sky in the mountain uplands and told everyone he had seen a unicorn. Or the same could have happened with an Arab or some other native of Africa at the sight of a gazelle. And thus we can have a perfectly 'natural' explanation of how the unicorn myth began."

Rüdiger Robert Beer, *Unicorn: Myth and Reality*

Ctesias's ass.

Or had it?

It is historical fact that a military genius named Genghis Khan marched his army into India. He conquered three cities there: Peshawar, Melikpur, and Lahore. Then he and his army turned back before they reached their objective of taking control of all India. Why?

The Beginnings of a Mystery

It is possible—even probable—that Genghis Khan had heard of unicorns before one confronted him in India. He may have associated one-horned creatures with the powerful Buddhist religion, which had begun in India in the sixth century B.C. If he had heard the Buddhist legend in which a gazelle (a small antelope) listens on bended knees to the Master's sermon, he may also have heard that it had a single horn between its ears. This set the creature apart from others of its kind since antelopes have two horns. The gazelle's horn was seen as a symbol of Nirvana, a heavenly state that is above all suffering and desire. A one-horned animal then—real or symbolic—was respected, and perhaps feared, long before Genghis Khan's time.

Perhaps the warrior lord saw an ordinary gazelle from the side view only. Such a view would make the animal appear to have but one horn. Perhaps he saw a mountain sheep, again in profile only. Such mountain creatures do bend down on their "knees."

Perhaps the khan saw neither of these, but instead saw an animal described centuries before by a man who had spent some time in the East. Around 400 B.C. a Greek named Ctesias returned to his native land after serving the king of Persia for seventeen years. While in the court of King Darius II, Ctesias listened as travelers told tales of distant lands. When he returned home, he wrote about the things he had heard and seen. One of his stories was about a marvelous one-horned animal. Ctesias wrote:

There are in India certain wild asses which are as large as horses and even larger. Their bodies are white, their heads dark red, and their eyes dark blue.

A unicorn hunt in India. These animals fit Ctesias's description.

They have a horn in the middle of the forehead that is about a foot and a half in length. . . . The base of this horn, for some two hands'-breadth above the brow, is pure white; the upper part is sharp and of a vivid crimson; and the remainder, or middle portion is black.

Was this the creature that Genghis Khan saw?

There was doubt in Ctesias's time—and there is doubt today. "Ctesias was confused," say the skeptics. Confusion was common in travelers' tales. In his *Encyclopedia of Monsters*, author Daniel Cohen says of Ctesias's text that "the basic animal being described is almost certainly the Indian rhinoceros, for the rhinoceros is the only one-horned animal in the world."

The rhinoceros was well-known, however. Those who respected Ctesias's writings said it did not seem reasonable that an intelligent man like Ctesias could mistake that sluggish, heavy animal for one with a horse-like body. A white body, at that, and with a tri-colored horn! They pointed out that Ctesias was a physician by profession, like his father and grandfather before him. As was fitting for such a family, his pedigree could be traced back to Aesculapius, the

Is it possible that this massive one-horned creature is the real unicorn?

god of medicine. This Greek writer was no ordinary traveler reciting stories heard around a campfire.

In his book, *Unicorn—Myth and Reality*, Rüdiger Robert Beer reports that for centuries natural scientists and artists based their work on Ctesias's commentary on the unicorn. Despite the doubts, the Greek doctor's description is still widely quoted by authors seeking the origins of belief in unicorns.

But what of Genghis Khan? Did this previously fearless leader become so frightened of a strange beast that he ordered his whole army to retreat?

Did he really believe this one-horned beast brought a warning that he had gone too far?

He might have. A ninth-century writer called Margoulis said, "It is universally held that the unicorn is a supernatural being and of auspicious omen." That is, this creature could tell what the future held. It would not be unusual then for even a strong leader to believe that such an animal was bringing him the message that he should not go on.

But no one knows if this is what really happened.

A medieval artist drew this collection of various kinds of unicorns.

What is known is that stories of one-horned animals having wonderful powers did not begin or end with Genghis Khan, Ctesias, or Buddhism. Even before the sixth century B.C. the unicorn was a central figure in Chinese legends, and through the years, stories of the existence of one-horned beasts have come from South Africa, Tibet, Scandinavia, Poland, Canada, and even the United States. In 1673 a Dr. Olfert Dapper wrote: ''On the Canadian border there are sometimes seen animals resembling horses, but with cloven hoofs [made of two parts], rough manes, a long straight horn upon the forehead, a curled tail like that of a wild boar [hog], black eyes, and a neck like that of the stag [deer].''

In some accounts the mysterious animals are shaped like bulls, in others like goats. Some are pure white and their coats shine like silver in the moonlight. Others have green shaggy hair, or yellow, or black. Some are huge, as big as mountains, while others are as small as dogs. The single horn may be short, thick,

A ''convention'' of animals from a medieval version of Aesop's fables.

Most people today think of a beautiful white horse-like creature when they think of a unicorn.

or curved, but it is the one feature that places all these varied creatures in the same category. They are all unicorns.

Today's Image of the Unicorn

But the popular image of the unicorn today is strikingly similar to the one described so long ago by Ctesias, only more beautiful, more wonderful to behold. Through the centuries the image of the unicorn has developed into a gleaming white horse-like creature with powerful shoulders, delicate legs and hoofs, a luxurious full mane, and a tail that flows out like a plume in the wind. The creature's eyes are large and dark and gentle, and poised above them is a single spiral horn, long and slender. When this gorgeous beast has passed by, the scent of cinnamon lingers in the air.

Who would want to doubt the reality of so lovely a creation? The more poetic the description, the more unreal the beast becomes. Yet in her book *The Unicorn*, author Nancy Hathaway observes that "as a phenomenon, the unicorn has been curiously tenacious [persistent], with many educated people coming to its defense—not just as story but as zoological fact." She goes on to say that perhaps unicorns existed at one time but are now extinct. This has happened to other animals—and some, such as the buffalo, were in danger of becoming extinct until people took steps to preserve them. Perhaps there was no way to protect the unicorn from extinction.

Hathaway suggests another possibility. Perhaps unicorns are mutants—animals born with a characteristic not common to their parents. In this case, a single horn. Could these occasional freaks of nature have given birth to others with a single horn, thus starting a new breed?

Perhaps unicorns—either mutants, or those that escaped extinction—still live somewhere far away— in the Mountains of the Moon at the source of the

The buffalo was in danger of becoming extinct until steps were taken to preserve it. Might the unicorn have become extinct because protective measures were not taken?

Nile River in Egypt, for instance, or in dark forests and deep valleys in the Far East. Perhaps.

But author Rüdiger Robert Beer does not think so. He starts his book with the words, ''The unicorn is as old as the knowledge of ancient China and still appears in contemporary literature, but it has never actually roamed the earth. It is a creature which never existed.''

Is Beer right? Or do the varying accounts and descriptions simply mean there are many varieties of unicorns?

Might the unicorn still exist in remote regions of the earth?

Two

Eastern Origins

"We may never know precisely when or where or how the legend of the unicorn began," says author Odell Shepard. There may well have been unicorns—or stories of them—long before recorded time. But as far as is known, stories from the Eastern countries are the beginnings of unicorn lore.

In Chinese tales of long ago there was a mysterious beast that had many forms. It was called the Ki-Lin. This creature had a single horn. Beyond this, little is known of this unicorn's appearance, as it was not described when the stories were written down. An obscure ninth-century writer remarked, "this animal does not figure among the barnyard animals. . . . We know that a certain animal with a mane is a horse and that a certain animal with horns is a bull. We do not know what the unicorn looks like." This did not prevent artists form coming up with images of the beast, however. Ancient Chinese drawings show the Ki, which is the male unicorn, the Lin, the female unicorn, and the combined male and female, the Ki-Lin (sometimes spelled k'i-lin, or simply ki-lin).

In these drawings the Ki has a smooth coat and legs and paws like a lion. The Lin has scales and cloven hoofs. Both have full manes that spread upward from the backs of their necks. When the male and female are combined in the Ki-Lin, some of their

Opposite page: The Japanese unicorn.

features change. For instance, they lose their manes, but gain a shaggy beard, and in place of one pointed horn the new creature has two horns, each of which has three prongs with rounded tips.

The Chinese Unicorn

This is but one description of the Ki-Lin, however. In a painting from the Ming Dynasty (1368-1644), the Ki-Lin resembles a bull with one horn curving forward. Yet two Chinese porcelain figurines from the K'ang Hsi period (1662-1773) are of creatures more dog-like in appearance with claws on their feet and with human mouths. A short horn grows between each figure's ears.

Colombian author Jorge Luis Borges in *The Book of Imaginary Beings* describes the Chinese unicorn in yet another way:

> The Unicorn is foremost [most important] of all the 360 creatures that live on land. It has the body of a deer, the tail of an ox, and the hooves of a horse.

Chinese artists imagined three species of the unicorn: the *Ki*, male (top), the *Lin*, female (middle), and the *Ki-Lin*, the combined form (right).

Its short horn, which grows out of its forehead, is made of flesh; its coat, on its back, is of five mixed colors, while its belly is brown or yellow. It is so gentle that when it walks it is careful not to tread on the tiniest living creature and will not even eat live grass but only what is dead . . .

The span of this animal's natural life is a thousand years.

Which is the true Ki-Lin? Perhaps they all are! In *The Lore of the Unicorn*, Odell Shepard names six different unicorns. They are the King, the Kioh Twan, the Poh, the Hiai Chai, the Too Jon Sheu, and the Ki-Lin. Shepard suggests they may all derive from a single original.

In the Beginning . . .

Chinese writers say the Ki-Lin comes "from afar, presumably from heaven." But Shepard says it also "is supposed to spring from the centre of the earth and perhaps he was originally a representative of the earthy element as the phoenix represents fire, the dragon air, and the tortoise water." In Chinese myth these four animals all foretell future events.

The phoenix is a legendary bird that lived more than one life. It consumed itself by fire periodically, and a new young phoenix sprang from the ashes. The bird had brilliant colors, like the pheasant and

In Chinese mythology, the tortoise (above) represented water and the phoenix (below) represented fire. These were two of the four basic elements that were believed to make up all creation.

> "The unicorn legend is different from most superstitions in that it has lasted longer and has been shared by the most enlightened minds of all nations."
>
> Andrea Bacci, sixteenth century botanist and physician

> "Some of the myths about unicorns might be more than just myths."
>
> Otter G'Zell, developer of Lancelot, the modern goat-unicorn

peacock. Borges states that "in prehistoric times it visited the gardens and palaces of virtuous emperors as a visible token of celestial [heavenly] favor." Or so it was said. No one knows whether the phoenix was purely imaginary, or if its origin could be traced to a real, but extinct, bird.

The dragon, the second prophetic animal, was a divine creature that signified wisdom. For centuries it was the imperial emblem. The emperor's throne was called the Dragon Throne and his face was called the Dragon Face. It was said that when an emperor died, he ascended into heaven on the back of a dragon. This beast is usually considered to be imaginary, though dragons may possibly be traced back to the age of dinosaurs.

The third animal, the tortoise or turtle, was thought to be an image or model of the world. Its upper shell curved like the heavens, its lower shell was flat the way the Chinese at that time believed the earth to be. They read the future in the pattern on the tor-

To the Chinese, the dragon represented the element of air and the characteristic of wisdom.

toise shell. Fossils of marine animals indicate that turtles may well be ancient animals that escaped extinction, for they can still be seen today.

The Unicorn's Appeal

The unicorn—if what Borges says is correct—was the most important of all these creatures. Why this should be so he does not say. Nor is it known why the Chinese singled out these four creatures to represent the elements of earth, fire, air, and water. But of the four, the unicorn has the most appeal as a creature that still fascinates researchers today. If it never lived, it should have. Author Nancy Hathaway says "the unicorn seems possible, even probable— a creature so likely that it ought to exist."

Shepard says, "According to the testimony of Tse-Tche-t'ong-kien-kang-mou, the ki-lin was first seen in the year 2697 B.C., in the palace of the Emperor Hoang-ti, on which occasion it was a truthful prophet of national felicity [happiness]." The emperor must have been delighted to have had this indication that his reign would be a happy one. In Chinese culture the unicorn showed itself only on important occasions, and was a sign of good times to follow. However, its

In Chinese mythology, the unicorn may have represented the earth element.

appearance could also predict the birth or death of a great person.

One of the most famous happy occasions on which the unicorn appeared was before the birth of the great philosopher, Confucius.

A Special Baby Is Born

As with so many old tales there is more than one version. Hathaway's is typical. She tells how a young woman called Ching-tsae had been walking for some distance when she became tired. She stopped to rest in an ancient temple. As Ching-tsae sat in a cool dark corner she fell into a trance. From behind an altar, an animal with a single horn appeared. Like all Chinese, Ching-tsae knew the unicorn was a good omen, and she was not afraid.

The mysterious animal slipped a tiny piece of jade from its mouth into her hand. Then it lowered its head into her lap. For several hours Ching-tsae rested and stroked the unicorn's head. While she did this "the air shimmered like water and was filled with the scent of cinnamon."

At last Ching-tsae was ready to continue her journey. She pulled an embroidered white ribbon from her hair and tied it around the horn of the Ki-Lin. As she did this, Hathaway says, "she suddenly felt woozy; for a second her eyes closed, and the k'i'lin vanished."

Ching-tsae took the piece of jade home to her husband, Heih. On one side of the smooth green stone an inscription had been carved. Ching-tsae was so in awe of what had happened that she could only whisper what the words said: "The son of the essence of water shall succeed to the withering Chou [the ruler at the time] and be a throneless king."

It was clear to Ching-tsae and Heih that they had been singled out in some special way, yet they did not understand what the words meant. Ching-tsae returned to the temple many times, hoping the unicorn would again appear. Once she thought she saw something out of the corner of her eye, but when she whirled around to catch a glimpse of the wispy phantom, nothing was there; it was only silk fluttering in a sudden breeze.

In the winter a baby was born to Ching-tsae. She named it Confucius. From his earliest days the child showed unusual wisdom. He became a great teacher and philosopher, truly a ''king without a throne.''

In one version of the story some hunters kill a Ki-Lin seventy years later and find the bit of ribbon that Confucius's mother had tied around its horn.

In another version, Confucius sees the unicorn years later and knows it is predicting that he will die soon.

Again we have a story that appears to be a tangle of history and folklore. Like Genghis Khan, Confucius

Confucius, the great Chinese philosopher. His mother met a unicorn before he was born, an omen that told her that he would be special, as indeed he was. Many people today continue to heed Confucius's wisdom.

Confucius was truly ''a king without a throne.'' His wisdom ruled many people, but he never held political office nor ruled a country. And, like many unusually wise people, he was expelled from his country for his ideas.

is a figure from history. He lived about 551-479 B.C. People studied his wise sayings and lived by them. But was his future predicted by an animal with one horn? Did this animal, like an angel, come from heaven?

This is something that cannot be proved. Yet myths and legends arise out of grains of truth. For example, a story that a family tells around the dinner table may take on more drama each time it is told. New details and fragments of other incidents are combined. Finally no one remembers what actually happened. It is the same with history. Much depends on who is telling the story. Could this be the case with the account of Confucius's birth?

Whether the tale is true or a myth, it had lasting importance for the Chinese people. Shepard says that even today pictures of the Ki-Lin are often displayed in the rooms of Chinese women in the hope that their babies will grow to be great men. Pictures of the unicorn ''are also affixed to the red chair in which the bride is borne to her husband's house, and the gods that oversee the distribution of desirable babies are often depicted riding upon the ki-lin. To say of any man that a ki-lin appeared at the time of his birth is the highest form of flattery.''

The Chinese Ki-Lin, while neither beautiful nor graceful like the modern image of the unicorn, was a gentle creature. It was a good omen, for even when it foretold of a death, the one-horned animal was not the cause of the sad event. It was only the bearer of the message. This was not the case with the Ki-Lin's counterpart across the sea, in the neighboring country of Japan. In this island country some people had reason to avoid an encounter with a ferocious beast with one horn.

The Kirin

In an old Japanese pen drawing, the Japanese unicorn, called the kirin, had the body of a bull with

Eastern people knew many one-horned creatures. This is *King*, the one-horned stag.

shaggy shoulder hair and eyes that stared out from under heavy brows. Although it too had other forms, like that of a deer or a goat, its eyes were always intent and threatening. It may well have been a creature to fear, for the kirin had the uncanny ability to detect right from wrong.

When Japanese judges presided in court, they decided most questions of guilt and innocence themselves. They had no trouble settling minor disputes, such as who was at fault when an injury was sustained while riding in a carriage, or what was to be done about a tomb that was not built to specifications. But when the case was a serious one involving a death, the judges sometimes did not entirely trust their own judgment. At those times they would call in the kirin.

The kirin always knew who was guilty and who was innocent. And its judgment was unsparing. It would stand very still, fix its eyes upon the guilty person, and then pierce him through the heart with its horn.

The Japanese unicorn, or kirin, could detect guilt and would punish the guilty with death.

Another Eastern variety of unicorn, the *Sz*, a one-horned Malaysian "sword-ox."

Stories such as these from China and Japan have a definite mythical quality. Did the storytellers expect their listeners to believe these tales? Perhaps—perhaps not. The tale of Confucius's unicorn is lovely to listen to and could easily be regarded as just a fairy tale, but for the fact that the idea of a one-horned creature became so solid a fixture in predicting births and deaths.

Perhaps the tale of the kirin was repeated as a warning: The guilty will surely be punished.

Whatever the reasons, the unicorn was an important part of oriental culture.

From another Eastern country, to the south and west of China, comes another tale, one that could very easily be believed. Anthony Shepherd recounts it in *The Flight of the Unicorns.*

The Twins and the Karkadann

One morning very early, Shepherd writes, a young man left his home in the desert of northern Arabia. He took with him a camel, a bow and arrow, and a small sack of provisions. Only his twin brother knew his intentions, and he was sworn to secrecy, for the young hunter was planning to kill a karkadann, a vicious brute with one black horn protruding from its forehead. The karkadann's voice was said to be so terrible that when it bellowed, the birds flew away.

No wonder this one-horned beast was feared by all living creatures and left thoroughly alone unless one had very good reasons for tracking it down. If the young man's family knew of his plans to seek the creature, they would surely have stopped him from going on such a dangerous mission.

When the man had been gone for three, then four days, his brother at home began to worry. Finally he too took a camel and set out across the sands. After a while he came upon his brother's leather sack in a puddle of dry brown blood. He fell to his knees, praying for help.

The karkadann, as pictured in a thirteenth-century Arabic manuscript.

When he arose he saw on the horizon the karkadann. This time it had the form of a graceful antelope, whose single horn curved over its back. And there—across its back—was draped the young hunter. The animal tossed its head, trying to dislodge the man, but it could not, for it had run its sharp horn through the man's thigh. Thus impaled, the hunter lay moaning in pain.

The twin aimed his bow and arrow at the beast, but did not shoot for fear of hitting his brother. Instead he waited until evening and hid in the tall grass. When morning came, he crept up on the animal as it grazed, and with his dagger, stabbed the creature between the ribs. It fell, screeching, blew out its sour breath, and died.

The Magic of the Karkadann

The second twin helped his wounded brother off the horn and bound his bleeding leg. They cut off the beast's horn and took it with the rest of the carcass back to their settlement. There, amidst joyful shouts of greeting, the fat of the karkadann was rubbed on the grandfather's aching knuckles and hips. He felt great relief. The meat of the animal was used to get rid of the demons that had been haunting the sleep of the twins' sister. And the horn was made into a flute to charm sheep and snakes. When not used to

Detail of a page from an Arabic manuscript showing Alexander the Great battling with a one-horned creature.

make enchanting music the horn served as a talisman [good-luck charm] against the bite of the dreaded scorpion. This was a valuable animal indeed.

Anthony Shepherd believes the unicorn of fable was actually the oryx, an antelope native to Arabia. If so, the adventure tale could have been based on a true story. Shepherd says, "The bedouin [desert dwellers] considered that a man who [killed] an oryx took on its virtues, which were those of courage, strength, and endurance. By eating it he became bursting with those desirable qualities." There were even more reasons for killing the beast, however. Besides the uses the bedouin in the story found for the karkadann he killed, Shepherd says the skin was used for leather and the face skin was prized as a cover for a rifle butt. A properly cured skin would bring a high price in the market.

The oryx inhabited a part of Arabia known as the "Empty Quarter," an area lacking in food, water, and shade. To come upon any animal there was a rare

The oryx, a graceful antelope. Seen from the side, it sometimes appears to have a single horn. Could the Arabian karkadann, or unicorn, really be an oryx?

thing, so when Douglas Carruthers, an authority on the oryx, came upon a whole herd around 1909 or 1910, he was surprised at his luck. He described his first sighting of the animal:

> I found, not as I expected, one solitary oryx, but a whole herd, bulls and cows and their little ones running beside them. It was a weird and ghostly sight in the gathering dusk. They seemed to be phantom beasts moving in a silent and supernatural world.

This and similar passages that mention seemingly "phantom" beasts and a "supernatural world," suggest the feeling of a fairy tale in what would otherwise be a straightforward account of a hunt in the wild. It is easy to see how the story could become fictionalized and the animal become one-horned. Shepherd gives convincing reasons for why he believes some people reported the oryx as having a single horn. He says, "An oryx seen sideways appears

A gentle, fawn-like unicorn from a Persian manuscript.

to have only one horn. It may be, although there are no reports of this, that some of the animals have lost a horn in battle, or through some mischance—indeed there may have been cases when an oryx has been born with only one—but this is conjecture and no more.''

Was the unicorn a real creature that walked the earth, or was it a spirit—or was it both?

Stories from the East must have stirred the imaginations of Europeans who wanted to believe that somewhere there were creatures that could cure illnesses, chase out demons, and protect them from such evils as the bites of scorpions. Were these people foolish to believe, and to have hope? Perhaps they were no more foolish than those today who carry a rabbit's foot for good luck, or use lanolin [wool grease from a sheep] in ointments and cosmetics.

People have always had "magical" talismans, items that are thought to provide something beyond the ordinary—a rabbit's foot or a four-leaf clover for luck, a bottle of "snake oil" for health—a piece of unicorn horn for protection.

Three

Rumor or Reality?

Hunting down the facts about unicorns is like hunting down the unicorn itself—an almost impossible task—for capturing a unicorn is like trying to capture a cloud. Who knows what is fact and what is fantasy? One way to ferret out the truth is to turn to those who seem to have some greater knowledge than the average person. In ancient times such a person was Aristotle, the most famous of the Greek philosophers.

Aristotle's Theory

Aristotle, who lived from 384 to 322 B.C., was a man who accumulated facts and observations, which, according to Funk and Wagnall's Encyclopedia, "were to a great extent the beginnings of physical science." He was the founder of the deductive science of logic, and the existence of a unicorn, from its physical description at least, was logical.

Aristotle no doubt heard the stories from the East and he had read Ctesias's works that described the ass-like unicorn in India. The philosopher considered the information he gleaned from such accounts and concluded that unicorns did exist. He explained how it was possible for such an animal to be single-horned.

Hoofs and claws, said Aristotle, consist of the same substance as horn. The ass has solid hoofs, not cloven ones like those of a goat. Thus a goat, with its cloven hoofs, has two horns. But the ass, whose

The truth of the beautiful and mysterious unicorn is difficult to track down.

The great Greek philosopher Aristotle believed that the unicorn could exist, but he did not believe in the magical powers attributed to it.

solid hoofs use more horny substance, has less material for forming horns, and only one horn grows from its head.

As for the rest of what Ctesias had written, Aristotle was skeptical. Ctesias, besides describing the appearance of the wild ass, wrote:

> The dust filed from this [unicorn] horn is administered in a potion as a protection against deadly drugs. Those who drink out of these horns, made into drinking vessels, are not subject, they say, to convulsions or the holy disease [epilepsy]. Indeed, they are immune even to poisons if, either before or after swallowing such, they drink wine, water, or anything else from these beakers.

But Aristotle was too much of a scientist to believe something that sounded so much like magic.

A Unicorn with a Curly Tail

According to author Rüdiger Robert Beer, another Greek, Megasthenes, who "moved in royal circles and conversed with sages," visited India about 333 B.C. He recorded what he learned there in four books, together called *Indika*. They were the most complete account of India then known to the Greeks. He told of a unicorn that he had heard of through the Brahmans, people of the highest religious and social caste of India. They spoke of the cartazoon, which was similar to Ctesias's one-horned ass. It was the size of a horse and had a mane. Its coat was dun-colored (dull brownish-gray), not white, but it had hoofs that "were without distinct segments, being of one solid piece." Its horn was only of one color—black, like that of the horrible karkadann of Arabia. And this horn was "extremely sharp and impregnably strong." Megasthenes added that the tail of this cartazoon was "as curly as a pig's!" Its voice was unpleasant, an "exceedingly raucous bray" (a loud, harsh sound usually made by a donkey). And finally, a new detail to add to the growing fund of knowledge about unicorns: Megasthenes said the unicorn had spirals on its horn. This last trait became a classic part of future descriptions of fabulous one-horned beasts.

Megasthenes must have heard the arguments that the only known single-horned animal was the rhinoceros, since he devoted a separate chapter specifically to this creature. In it he distinguished the cartazoon from the rhinoceros by its habits. The rhinoceros, he said, engages in atrocious fights, usually with elephants, over grazing grounds. The cartazoon, in contrast, was "remarkably gentle." It was solitary by nature.

Megasthenes was sure the cartazoon was rarely seen because it kept to itself in the impassable mountains of India. However, he said young unicorns were frequently brought to the royal palaces and displayed in festivals. What happened to the young unicorns when the festivals were over? Megasthenes did not say.

These writings would be more solid evidence of the existence of the unicorn if Megasthenes had seen the animal himself, but as author Odell Shepard points out, "scholarship consisted largely in the discovery, balancing, and recording of what others had said." This method of passing on information was used also by Gaius Plinius Secundus (about A.D. 23-79), better known as Pliny the Elder.

This Roman statesman, soldier, and author compiled an encyclopedia of nature and art in thirty-seven

"They say that it is impossible to capture this animal alive."

Pliny the Elder, first century AD philosopher

"You don't have to have a golden bridle to catch a unicorn; that part's the fairy tale. You need only to be pure of heart."

The elder hunter in Peter S. Beagle's *The Last Unicorn*

The Indian cartazoon had a black horn, a curly pig's tail, and a terrible bray.

Pliny's unicorn had elephant-like feet!

books. This *Historia Naturalis* is the only one of his works which has been preserved. He claimed that it contained twenty thousand important facts, extracted from about two thousand volumes by a hundred authors.

Pliny's unicorn had "a stag's head, elephant's feet, and a boar's tail, the rest of its body being like that of a horse. . . . One black horn two cubits long [about three feet long] projects from the middle of the forehead. This animal, they say, cannot be taken alive."

"Here," says Shepard, "is a sober account written by a serious-minded man." Pliny made no claims for magical powers for the creature he described. Shepard says this reference to the unicorn is important chiefly because "for more than a thousand years Pliny's beliefs about animals were the beliefs of almost every reader . . . in Europe."

Aelian

Those who have researched the origins of unicorn lore often mention another influential Roman writer. Claudius Aelianus—known as Aelian—lived from A.D. 170-235. In his *On the Nature of Animals* he told of a unicorn that matched Ctesias's, except for one detail. Aelian said a unicorn had a black ankle-bone. Ctesias said it was the color of cinnabar [red]. In addition Ctesias had said that "other asses, both tame and wild, in fact all animals with solid hoofs, are

Pliny the Elder looking at a bestiary. He described a unicorn in one volume of his huge and influential natural history.

without ankle-bones.'' The wild ass, though, had ''the most beautiful'' ankle-bone Ctesias had ever seen. Since ankle-bones were used for making dice, this was one more use for a bit of the precious unicorn—if it could ever be found.

Everything that Megasthenes, Pliny, and Aelian had written could be classified as hearsay. Hearsay is evidence based not on a witness's personal knowledge, but on matters told him by another. Hearsay is not proof. Was there no one who had actually seen with his own eyes the elusive creature that was so real, yet so magical?

An Eyewitness Appears

In the first century A.D., Apollonius of Tyana journeyed from his native Greece to India. There, said Apollonius, he *saw* the one-horned wild asses described by Ctesias. And now he could believe what he had heard and read!

Like Pliny, Apollonius was a sober-minded man. He could believe what his eyes had seen, but as to the powers of this fabulous creature he was not so sure. When told that the rulers of India drank from alicorn cups [made from unicorn horn] and were thus protected against sickness and poison, he must have shaken his head in wonder, for he said, ''I should have believed it if I had found that the kings of this country were immortal.''

Here at last was a first-hand account! Whether Apollonius spoke the truth, there is no way of knowing. But he was, at least, willing to state that he had personal knowledge that the mysterious beast existed.

Even so, statements such as Apollonius's did not settle anything. For centuries the unicorn and its lore lived merely from book to book.

Then something happened that won the unicorn a place in the hearts of men and women for centuries to come.

Apollonius of Tyana claimed to have actually seen the one-horned asses described by Ctesias.

Four

The Spiritual Unicorn

The idea of the unicorn did not really flourish in the ancient Western world until the third century. Then the one-horned creature found its way into the Bible, the book to which Christians and Jews turn for spiritual guidance. Now the unicorn attained a legitimacy not before accorded it.

There are seven clear references to the unicorn in the King James Version of the Bible. All of them occur in the Old Testament. These passages read as follows:

God brought them out of Egypt; he hath as it were the strength of the unicorn. — Numbers 23:22

His glory is like the firstling of his bullock, and his horns are like the horns of unicorns; with them he shall push the people together to the ends of the earth. — Deuteronomy 33:17

Save me from the lion's mouth; for thou hast heard me from the horns of unicorns. — Psalm 22:21

He maketh them [the cedars of Lebanon] also to skip like a calf; Lebanon and Sirion like a young unicorn. — Psalm 29:5-6

But my horn shalt thou exalt like the horn of the unicorn; I shall be anointed with fresh oil. — Psalm 92:10

Opposite page: The unicorn is often seen in medieval religious art. In this Spanish illuminated painting, the unicorn is shown to be symbolic of Christ.

Scholars don't know what kind of animal the biblical unicorn, *Re'em*, was. Might it have been a wild ox, a rhinoceros, or an oryx?

And the unicorns shall come down with them, and the bullocks with their bulls; and their land shall be soaked with blood, and their dust made fat with fatness. — Isaiah 34:7

Will the unicorn be willing to serve thee, or abide in thy crib?

Canst thou bind the unicorn with his band in the furrow? or will he harrow the valleys after thee?

Wilt thou trust him because his strength is great? or wilt thou leave thy labour to him?

Wilt thou believe him, that he will bring home thy seed, and gather it into thy barn? — Job 39:9-12

"One thing is evident in these passages," says author Odell Shepard. "They refer to some actual animal of which the several writers had vivid if not clear impressions." In each case the animal referred to was a wild beast of strength, ferocity, and unconquerable spirit. If not the unicorn, then what animal was this?

Could the existence of the unicorn be doubted if the Bible, the word of God, attested to it? It could be if the reader of the Biblical passages knew that when the Hebrew Bible was translated into Greek in the third century the translators took the Hebrew word *Re'em* and translated it *monokeros*, or *one-horned*. In the Latin version, *monokeros* became *unicornis*. The problem is, no one knows what animal the Re'em was. Some scholars believe it was the wild ox. Others say the rhinoceros. Still others say it was the oryx, the large straight-horned African antelope, which, seen from the side, appears to have one horn.

For most people these theories were not worth discussing. The Bible named a creature—a unicorn—therefore it existed. And they had only to turn to the Old Testament to find a story that included a marvelous one-horned beast.

Daniel's Dream

In the book of Daniel, God gave special learning and wisdom to four children of Judah. Among them was Daniel, who understood all visions and dreams. He knew secrets and could read the future. Because of his visions, Daniel's sleep was often troubled.

One night while he was sleeping on the ground, the winds blew around him, and he became more restless than usual. This night he dreamed he was at the River Ulai. By its bank stood a ram [a male sheep] with two horns, one larger than the other. As it stood there, the ram grew. With every breath it took its grey sides expanded, to the west, the north, and the south. It looked invincible.

Then a unicorn appeared. It was shaped like a goat, with a goat-like beard, but with one mighty horn. Its eyes were red with rage. It stood above the curve of the river, then lowered its horn and stalked across the river toward the ram. As author Nancy Hathaway retells the story:

> With its every footstep, ripples swelled outward and broke against the banks like tidal waves. The wind whipped around its horn and sounded low, like thunder, like the call of whales: and lightning splintered from the tip of its horn.
>
> The unicorn pursued the ram until the two animals were facing each other. The ram backed up, the unicorn pushed forward. Finally the two beasts stood still. They both lowered their horns and stamped upon the ground with their hoofs. The unicorn lunged at the ram's head; with a swoop of its sword-like horn, it severed the horns of the ram, knocked the beast into the river and trampled it. The muddy waters of the Ulai swirled scarlet.
>
> Then the unicorn began to grow. Its single horn, now tipped with blood, broke off, and in its place there sprung up four smaller horns. Out of one of them sprouted yet another, which grew greater than the others until it touched the heavens. Stars plummeted in a veil of sparks and the ground was covered with the dust of comets.

Then, as the story goes, the angel Gabriel appeared, and with a voice that made the earth quake,

''What really insured the survival of the unicorn concept into modern times was its mention in the Bible.''

Daniel Cohen, *The Encyclopedia of Monsters*

''With the unicorn thus already in the Garden of Eden, why is it not found in the Biblical events that follow?''

Rüdiger Robert Beer, *Unicorn: Myth and Reality*

An illustration of Daniel's dream, from a Spanish miniature
painted more than a thousand years ago.

Adam, Eve, and a unicorn in the Garden of Eden, based on an old illustration.

which means naturalist. There could have been more than one naturalist, but as the stories began with the words, ''The Physiologus says,'' the whole collection came to be regarded as the work of one author called Physiologus. Early preachers relied on the stories to teach scriptural lessons. Later the stories were copied, though the Bible lessons were omitted. Thus, the image of the unicorn as a goat-like creature, very fierce for its size, spread throughout the Christian world.

Such books came to be known as Bestiaries, or books of animals. T.J. Elliott, who translated *A Medieval Bestiary* from a book thought to have been written in the thirteenth century, observes that ''the Bestiary purports to be a scientific compendium [a brief summary of a larger work], [but] . . . it really tells us more about human beings and the history of ideas than about natural history.''

In the minds of some people, the unicorn became more than a worldly creature, or one used to teach moral lessons. It took on a deeper meaning.

Because of the unicorn's strength, purity, and power, it was, in medieval times, a symbol for Jesus Christ, the central figure of the Christian religion. Its single horn was said to signify the unity of Christ and God the Father; its fierceness and defiance of the hunter were to remind Christians that no kingdom or ruler could control the Messiah (Christ) against His will. Gospel manuscripts of the ninth century show the Virgin Mary with the unicorn on her lap.

Yet the unicorn could stand for both good and evil. In the thirty-fourth chapter of the book of Isaiah, unicorns appear as a symbol for the heathens, those who were non-believers. Pope Gregory the Great called the Prince of Darkness (the devil) a unicorn.

But St. Ambrose, bishop of Milan, Italy, in the fourth century, asked, "Who then has one horn,

Pope Gregory the Great viewed the unicorn as a symbol of evil.

unless it be the only-begotten son, the unique word of God, which has been next to God from the very beginning?'' Although St. Ambrose showed by this statement that he considered the unicorn to be a fitting symbol for Jesus Christ, the bishop had serious doubts about the unicorn as a real animal, for he also said, ''The unicorn itself, so experts say, is not to be found among generations of beasts.'' Author Rüdiger Robert Beer believes that St. Ambrose's doubt about the reality of unicorns led him to develop his spiritual interpretation of the unicorn as representing Christ.

The question remained unanswered. Was the unicorn a *real* animal? If it was a living creature that God had created and placed with the other animals in the Garden of Eden, what had become of it? A story based on one in the Old Testament suggests an answer—or two, depending on the version told.

St. Ambrose viewed the unicorn as symbolic of Jesus Christ.

The Flood

The Bible says there was a time when the earth became so corrupt and violent that God wanted to begin anew. But not everything was to be destroyed. A voice from the heavens instructed a man named Noah to build an ark. This was to be a seaworthy ship, capable of holding two of every creature on earth.

With the help of his three sons, Noah built such a craft. When it was done, he took aboard one male and one female of all the animals, but of the birds he took seven of each so that later they could spread seeds across the face of the earth. All the animals, from the flea to the elephant, filed up the wooden gangplank.

The rains came, and the ark rose with the water. Inside the ark the animals rocked in the darkness as the waves pounded the ship. When the flood was finally over and the land was dry they left the ark. But the unicorn was not among them.

According to a Jewish folktale, the unicorn was so rambunctious as the ark was being loaded that Noah

There are several legends about unicorns and the Great Flood of Noah. One says the unicorns were too obnoxious to be allowed to stay on the ark; another says they declined to board it with the other animals.

became irritated with it. The beautiful creature prodded the other animals when it was eventually allowed on board and demanded more space. Noah, his patience at an end, ordered the unicorn to leave the ark. It galloped off, never to be seen again.

If this tale is true, the unicorn drowned in the flood that covered the earth.

Another version of the story says that isn't the way it happened. The unicorn was huge, bigger than any other animal. It was just too big to fit on the ark. For forty days and forty nights the unicorn swam in the rising seas. When it grew tired it rested its horn on the ark. When the rains stopped the unicorn trotted off to live the solitary life it preferred.

The first story suggests that the unicorn is extinct, like the dinosaur. In the second version, it still lives somewhere—apart from all other creatures.

But where? Are there regions on the earth where animals can go and be hidden from civilization? There may be.

Some respected scientists believe a huge hairy creature commonly called Bigfoot may be living in parts of the northwestern American continent, or in isolated mountains of Asia.

Could unicorns have found an equally isolated place? Do they still live today? Or do they exist only as religious symbols and in the minds of those who *want* to believe in them?

We know that dinosaurs once existed but are now extinct, and we have rumors that unusual creatures, like Bigfoot, still inhabit the earth in hidden places. What about unicorns? Do they fit one of these two categories?

Five

Medieval Times

By the Middle Ages, or medieval times (approximately A.D. 500 to 1500), the unicorn had been established as a creature of religious significance. Whether it was a real animal was questionable, but to people in Europe, it seemed possible that such an animal existed. From the shores of the Orient and the deserts of Arabia, stories of a one-horned animal continued to arrive in western Europe. They came by way of merchants who brought silk, spices, and other exotic items to kings and queens in their castles. In the lonely monasteries and the thatched huts of the poor, tales of fabulous one-horned beasts were repeated and believed.

"People of the Middle Ages had no more reason to doubt the existence of the unicorn than they did to doubt the existence of the elephant or the camel, which they had also never seen, and which in certain ways seemed far less likely creatures than the unicorn," says author Nancy Hathaway in her book *The Unicorn*. Indeed, if an elephant had a nose so long it could pick up food with it and deposit that food in its mouth, and a camel had a hump in which it stored nourishment for several days, why could not there also be a creature whose single spiral horn had extraordinary powers?

In the marketplace of the Middle Ages, people purchased daily necessities as well as silks, spices, and other exotic items—including unicorn horn.

If strange creatures like the elephant and the camel could exist, why not the unicorn?

Therefore tales told of people who claimed they had actually seen unicorns were not considered too unusual. Many of the tales centered around a wonderful place where unicorns were plentiful.

Glimpses of the Elusive Beast

"About the middle of the twelfth century," writes Sabine Baring-Gould in *Curious Myths of the Middle Ages*, "a rumor circulated through Europe that there reigned in Asia a powerful Christian Emperor, Presbyter Johannes." This Priest-King, it was said, had broken the power of the barbarians who were fighting against the Christian Crusaders.

At this time, Mongol hordes were rushing in upon the West, with Russia, Poland, Hungary, and the eastern provinces of Germany suffering from the invasion. So, in the hope of saving Christianity, Pope Alexander III determined to join forces with this mysterious person who had become popularly known as Prester John.

According to Baring-Gould, on September 27, 1177, the Pope wrote the Priest-King a letter. Alexander entrusted it to his physician, Philip, who was to deliver it in person. Philip left on his mission, but never returned.

The mysterious and magnificent Prester John, who claimed to live in a paradise. Some people said that unicorns also lived there.

Trying to spread and save their Christian heritage, the crusaders battled fiercely against Saracens and Mongols.

About this same period, however, a letter from somewhere in the Far East arrived in Constantinople for the emperor, Manuel Comnenus. Similar letters were supposedly sent to Alexander III, to Louis VII of France, and to the King of Portugal. The letters told of a kingdom free from thievery, lies, and all vice. It was a place filled with miracles of nature, and the king who ruled over all had a palace of ebony and crystal.

This king was Prester John, and he had written the letters himself—or so it was said. Though the letters gave no promise of help to Alexander and his Christian subjects, they described a wondrous kingdom:

> Our land streams with honey and is overflowing with milk. In one region grows no poisonous herb . . . nor can any poisonous animals exist in it, or injure anyone. . . . Our land is the home of elephants, dromedaries, camels, crocodiles, meta-collinarum, cametennus, tensevetes, wild asses, white and red lions . . . and of nearly all living animals.

Surely in a kingdom so marvelous, the wild asses must be those with one horn that Ctesias had mentioned. There was ample room for such creatures, as Prester John's empire was enormous, with seventy-

"Where did they come from, where have they gone, were they ever here at all? The truth is, no one knows for certain. But here's what I believe: wherever else they may have come from unicorns live inside the true believer's heart. Which means that as long as we can dream, there will be unicorns."

Bruce Coville, *The Unicorn Treasury*

"Is it then possible that the last of these monsters survived long enough to be contemporary with the first man, to be observed, remembered, and the remembrance developed? . . . Their memory might well have been preserved by distant descendants of the men who had actually seen them, by people far removed both in space and time from the last haunt of the last [creature] itself."

Peter Lum, *Fabulous Beasts*

two separate kingdoms under his rule. One of them apparently was in the vicinity of the Garden of Eden, for in another passage he informed the western world that,

> in a certain land subject to us . . . at the foot of Mount Olympus bubbles up a spring which changes its flavour hour by hour, night and day, and the spring is scarcely three days' journey from Paradise, out of which Adam was driven. If anyone has tasted thrice [three times] of the fountain, from that day he will feel no fatigue, but will as long as he lives be as a man of thirty years.

In a land so remarkable, anything was possible!

When a number of missionaries and ambassadors of peace were sent among the eastern barbarians who remained in Europe after their unsuccessful invasion, it soon became evident to the Europeans that there was no mighty Christian empire existing in central

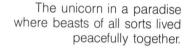

The unicorn in a paradise where beasts of all sorts lived peacefully together.

Asia. This did nothing to squelch the rumor of Prester John's court, however. Baring-Gould writes, ''Vulgar superstition or conviction is not . . . to be upset by evidence, and the locality of the monarchy was merely transferred by the people to [eastern] Africa.'' They fixed upon Abyssinia, now Ethiopia, as the seat of the famous Priest-King.

For a long while travelers sought Prester John's kingdom in vain. But it came as no surprise when Edward Webbe, an English adventurer, claimed to have found unicorns and the kingdom of Prester John while journeying through Africa:

> I have seen in a place like a park adjoining Prester John's Court, three score and seventeen unicornes and eliphants all alive at one time, and they were so tame that I have played with them as one would play with young Lambes.

Other travelers had visited monarchs who claimed to have received gifts of unicorn horn from Prester John. King John II of Portugal and Vasco da Gama, the Portuguese navigator, also spoke of Prester John's Court, thus reinforcing the beliefs of those who stayed at home in Europe.

Marco Polo, the famous Italian explorer, maintained that there was a mighty Christian monarch in Abyssinia, but that he was not Prester John. Marco

Several medieval travelers claimed to have seen unicorns.

Explorers Marco Polo (left), and Vasco da Gama (right) gave conflicting reports about Prester John.

John of Hesse claimed to have seen unicorns purifying poisoned water.

Polo said Prester John reigned in splendor somewhere in the dim Orient. Prester John was as elusive as the unicorn.

But reports of unicorn sightings came not only from explorers, adventurers, and Prester John's Court. Sightings came also from men of the Church.

John of Hesse

In 1389 a priest from Germany, named John of Hesse visited the Holy Land on the east coast of the Mediterranean Sea. He wrote:

> Near the field of Helyon there is a river called Marah, the water of which is very bitter, into which Moses struck his staff and made the water sweet so that the Children of Israel might drink. And even in our times, it is said, venomous animals poison that water after the setting of the sun, so that the good animals cannot drink of it; but in the morning, after the sunrise, comes the unicorn and dips his horn into the stream, driving the poison from it so that the good animals can drink there during the day. This I have seen myself.

Who could doubt such testimony?

Stories such as this one by John of Hesse may have given rise to the belief that unicorn horn, if it could purify water, could purify food also. Anyone who had read Ctesias's works already knew that a person who

A unicorn dips its horn into water, removing or neutralizing the venom of various poisonous creatures.

drank from vessels made of unicorn horn would not be poisoned, and that scrapings from the horn would cure sickness. No more evidence was necessary.

Unicorn horn was much sought after, and it became a part of medieval life.

Unicorn Power

These were dangerous times in which to live. Royalty was constantly in fear of being poisoned by enemies, so when a peddler arrived with what he said was a piece of unicorn horn he was welcomed into the palace. Any king rich enough to purchase a whole horn placed it on his dinner table where its mere presence would ensure the purity of the food he and his guests ate. If a horn was not available, a hoof from this wondrous creature would do. Author Rüdiger Robert Beer quotes some advice from a source unknown:

> Anyone who fears being poisoned should place a unicorn hoof beneath the plate containing his food or the mug holding his liquor. If warm food and drink are poisoned the hoof will make them effervesce [bubble]; if they are cold, it will make them steam. Thus one can detect whether they are poisoned or not.

Apparently, in some cases if the horn or hoof did not neutralize poison immediately, it at least warned of the danger.

Pieces of horn were fashioned into goblets, and knives were made with unicorn handles. But still some royalty died by poison. When this happened the surviving king or queen did not question the power of unicorn horn, or alicorn, as it was called. Instead they wondered if what they had purchased was *true* alicorn. Could the peddler have sold them a piece of horn from a goat or a bull instead of the real thing?

There was only one way to find out. Test it.

Testing the Horn

Several procedures were developed to determine whether a king had been duped. One of these involved

A necklace, supposedly made from unicorn horn. Items such as this were believed to protect the wearer.

# UNICORNS HORN

Now brought in Ufe for the Cure of Difeafes by an Experi enced DOCTOR, the AUTHOR of this Antidote.

A Moft Excellent Drink made with a true *Unicorns Horn*, which dotl Effectually Cure thefe Difeafes :

Further, If any pleafe to be fatisfied, they may come to the Doctor and view the *Horn.*

Viz. {
Scurvy, Old Ulcers,
Dropfie,
Running Gout,
Confumptions, Diftillations, Coughs
Palpitation of the Heart,
Fainting Fits, Convulfions,
Kings Evil, Rickets in Children,
Melancholly or Sadnefs,
The Green Sickneß, Obftructions,
}

And all Diftempers proceeding from a Cold Caufe.

The Ufe of it is fo profitable, that it prevents Difeafes and Infection by fortifying the Noble Parts, and powerfully expels what is an Enemy to Nature, preferving the Vigour, Youth, and a good Complexion to Old Age : The Virtue is of fuch force, as to refift an Injury from an unfound Bedfellow ; None can excel this, for it is joyned with the Virtue of a true *Unicorns Horn*, through which the Drink paffeth, and being impregnated therewith, it doth wonderfully Corroborate and Cure, drinking it warm at any time of the Day, about a quarter of a Pint at a time, the oftner the better, the Price is 2 s. the Quart.

2. Alfo as a preparative for this excellent Drink, and good againft the Difeafes above mentioned, and all Crudities in the Body, is ready prepared twelve Pils in a Box to be taken at three Dofes, according to Directions therewith given, the Price is 2 s. the Box.

3. Likewife he hath Admirable Medicines for the Cure of the POX. or Running of the Reins, with all Simptoms and Accidents thereto belonging, whether Newly taken or of long Continuance, and (by God's Blef fing) feures the Patient from the danger of the Difeafe prefently, and perfects the Cure with the greateft Speed and Secretie imaginable, not hindering Occafions, or going abroad : Whofoever makes Ufe of thefe Admirable Medicines, may have further Advice from the Doctor without Charge.

The Doctor Liveth in Hounfditch, *next Door to* Gun-Yard, *having a Back Door into the Yard, where any Patient may come pri*

A medieval advertisement selling unicorn horn, ''for the cure of diseases.''

taking a goblet carved out of alicorn and turning it upside down over two scorpions. If these poisonous members of the spider family died, it was true unicorn horn. If the scorpions lived, the goblet had been made from false alicorn.

A similar test was performed with two doves. Both birds were given arsenic, a poison. Then one of the doves was fed a brew of powdered horn. If the horn were truly unicorn, the bird would live. If not, both died.

Occasionally, a servant was instructed to drink poison to which powdered alicorn had been added. If he or she died—well—the conclusion was obvious.

Besides rendering poison ineffective, various parts of unicorns were highly prized for their medicinal qualities. Here again the Church contributed a ring of authority.

A Miraculous Cure

In the twelfth century, St. Hildegard of Bingen (1098-1179), the abbess of a nunnery, wrote down these directions for those who would guard against ill health:

> Take some unicorn liver, grind it up and mash with egg yolk to make an ointment. Every type of leprosy is healed if treated frequently with this ointment, unless the patient is destined to die or God intends not to aid him. For the liver of that animal has a good, pure warmth and the yolk is the most precious part of the egg and like a salve. Leprosy, however, comes frequently from black bile and from plethoric black blood. Take some unicorn pelt, from it cut a belt and gird it round the body, thus averting attack by plague or fever.
>
> Make also some shoes from unicorn leather and wear them, thus assuring ever healthy feet, thighs, and joints, nor will the plague ever attack those limbs.
>
> Apart from that, nothing else of the unicorn is to be used medically.

To a medical world using mysterious vegetable and animal extracts, portions of mummies, pieces of bone,

St. Hildegard of Bingen was convinced of the value of some parts of the unicorn in curing illness. Unlike most others, St. Hildegard did not prescribe use of the horn.

Above: Medieval monks working as pharmacists to create cures for illnesses. Unicorn horn was said to have been a valuable ingredient for many curatives. Below: Unicorns came to be used as symbols for apothecaries, or pharmacies, because of their connection with healing.

and the like to cure diseases and heal wounds, the use of unicorn was not strange. And since the phrase "unless the patient is destined to die or God intends not to aid him" was inserted in the remedy, no one could blame St. Hildegard if her methods did not work. If the phrase also meant that God worked directly through the unicorn, then these were powerful remedies indeed.

St. Hildegard's prescriptions did not include the use of the horn of the unicorn, but monks acquired pieces of alicorn and their monasteries treasured them as they would a holy relic. They scraped away bits of the horn, and mixed the powder thus obtained, not with egg yolk, but with oils to make a salve or with liquid to be drunk. Unicorn horn was prescribed to cure fever, fits, and the plague, as well as children's ailments, such as colic. According to Dr. Conrad Gesner (1516-1565), "this horn is useful and beneficial against epilepsy, pestilent fever, rabies, . . . and infection of other animals and vermin, and against the worms within the body from which children faint."

Dr. Gesner included this information in his bestiary published in Zurich, Switzerland in 1563. He explained that:

The potency of the unicorn is more curative forward near the tip than behind, and care should be taken to buy the whole or at any rate large chunks of the horn, so as to run less risk of trickery.

Dr. Gesner cautioned that if the piece of horn is ''easily crushed when you bite on it'' and not tough like true alicorn, fraud is clearly indicated, for it could be the horn of some other animal.

Although the doctor believed that ''genuine unicorn is good against all poison,'' he had doubts about the claim that sweat on the horn was a danger signal:

> It is also false and deceitful for them to say that where unicorn's horn is lying and poison comes into its vicinity, the unicorn will sweat; it may well be that sometimes it does sweat, just like other solid bodies such as stone and glass on which vapours and moistures can outwardly freeze and then vanish again, without poison being any reason for that. For that occurs also with the stone called serpentine which they say shows where poison is present, but that is not so.

Dr. Gesner was not alone in looking to science for explanations. When St. Hildegard was pressed to explain why unicorn was more powerful than the liver or hide of other animals, she attributed the creature's great strength to what it ate. She claimed the unicorn went once yearly into the country where the waters of paradise flow. There it sought out the best herbs and vegetables, ''pawed them loose from the soil and devoured them.'' The strength the animal acquired from doing this was evidently passed on to those who used its parts as medicine.

Alicorn and Vaccines

Another source—this one obscure, but recounted by author Odell Shepard in *The Lore of the Unicorn*—maintained that horned animals had a keen appetite for poisonous substances, both animal and vegetable.

''The belief that all horns have medicinal value and that this value is of a supernatural sort [has] lasted on, demonstrably, into modern times.''

Odell Shepard, *The Lore of the Unicorn*

''Now a belief in the value of powdered horn as an aphrodisiac seems restricted to Chinese quacks.''

Peter Costello, *The Magic Zoo*

"God himself must need be traduced [degraded by falsehoods], if there is no unicorn."

Edward Topell in *Historie of Four-Footed Beastes*, written in the 17th century

"We care for facts, and are comparatively careless about ultimate meanings; the Middle Ages were regardful of meanings and careless about facts."

Odell Shepard, *The Lore of the Unicorn*

This poison was drawn into their horns and concentrated in them. When all the poison that would ordinarily be distributed through two horns was forced into one, it was brought to a very strong focus. The one horn then carried off feebler poisons such as arsenic by virtue of its own more powerfully poisonous nature.

This line of thinking seems strange, but could it have been the forerunner of the scientific thought that later developed vaccines?

For instance, a smallpox vaccine was developed by an English physician, Edward Jenner, between 1796 and 1798: Jenner observed that milkmaids who had cowpox were immune to smallpox, a much more severe disease. Jenner injected a boy with cowpox, and later attempted to produce smallpox in the boy. The attempts were unsuccessful. From Jenner's experiments came the method of inoculating a person by placing a small amount of smallpox virus under a person's skin, thus causing a very slight case of the disease. The person recovers, and is thereafter immune to the dreaded disease.

Did a bit of poisonous alicorn act like a vaccine?

Whether there was any scientific basis for the powers credited to the unicorn has never been proved, but it was so popular a remedy that even doctors who

Edward Jenner, who developed the smallpox vaccine. Did alicorn work in a fashion similar to a vaccine?

Ambroise Paré, the great French surgeon, said that doctors used alicorn even if they did not believe it had true value. They used it because their patients demanded it.

didn't believe in it carried powders and chunks of horn supposedly from this special beast.

Ambroise Paré, a great French surgeon of the sixteenth century, said, "Physicians are frequently compelled to prescribe unicorn . . . because patients demand such remedies. For if it happened that a patient who had made a request were to die without receiving what he wanted, the family would expel such physicians and disparage them in gossip as 'quite out of touch.'"

Unicorn was expensive medicine, but rather than risk their reputations, the doctors gave in to their patients' wishes. The fragments and scrapings used by physicians were not nearly so costly as whole horns, however. In the first year of the reign of Queen Elizabeth I of England (1558), an inventory was taken at Windsor Castle. A unicorn horn was recorded with a value of 10,000 pounds, equivalent to about 150,000 dollars today.

By the 1500s there was some evidence that not all the horns sold throughout Europe came from a white horse-like animal that lived on land. It appeared that some slender spiral horns may have come from a creature of the sea.

The Sea-Unicorn

In an article in *Smithsonian* magazine in February 1980, Noel D. Vietmeyer tells how one explorer came upon an animal that Vietmeyer claims inspired ''the myth of the unicorn.''

The summer storm slashed out of the nearby Arctic so swiftly and violently that Martin Frobisher's three fragile ships were almost pulverized. With kneeling crews thanking God for deliverance, the trio of vessels limped to shelter in a vast, ice-spattered inlet on Baffin Island's southeastern corner. It was July 1577, and Frobisher was to get little farther in his search for an Atlantic-to-Pacific passage across the top of North America. The voyage so far had yielded few exciting discoveries, but here, on a small island in their inlet haven (now known as Frobisher

The narwhal, a dolphin-sized whale with a tremendously long tooth. Narwhal horn may have been commonly sold as unicorn horn.

Bay), some crew members found "a great dead fish." The fish was unlike any previously documented. It was "round like to a porpoise, being about twelve feet long . . . having a horn of two yards long growing out of the snout or nostrils."

The horn was of such pure ivory, so straight, and of such a perfectly tapered and spiraled shape that Frobisher instinctively knew he had made a historic discovery: a marine species of unicorn.

It was widely believed that for every terrestrial creature there was a marine counterpart. This notion is evident even today in such names as sea-horse and sea-lion. So Frobisher's crew accepted the sea-unicorn quite readily. But to dispel any doubts as to what they had found, they performed a test for false unicorn horn. They put some supposedly poisonous spiders into the hollow horn. The spiders died. That was all Frobisher needed to know. He wrote, "This horn . . . may truly be thought to be the sea-unicorn." He proudly presented the gleaming ivory lance to Queen Elizabeth.

Thus Frobisher reported to Europe the existence of the narwhal, a dolphin-sized whale. Could others before him have been selling narwhal horn?

That would come as no surprise, since this mammal's horn is wondrous—and abundant too! The horn is "seven to nine feet" in length. However, it really is not a horn at all, but a tooth that juts out through its lips in a spiraling motion. No one has discovered what the purpose of the tooth is. In fact, despite pictures taken from helicopters proving the existence of the narwhal, this mammal is almost as little known today as it was in Frobisher's time.

The knowledge that unicorn horns might come from the sea as well as from animals that lived on land did little to shake the faith in the power of alicorn. But as narwhal "horns" became increasingly available, alicorn lost some of its monetary value. The price of unicorn by the half-ounce in Frankfurt, Ger-

Many people thought that every land creature had a counterpart in the sea. Even today we have such pairs as the horse and the seahorse.

Top: Robert III, King of Scotland, made unicorns a part of the official seal of Scotland. Bottom: James I became king of both Scotland and England. He combined the Scottish unicorn with the British lion for the new British coat of arms.

many, went from 64 florins in 1612, to only 4 florins in 1669. However powdered unicorn horn remained on a British list of effective drugs into the eighteenth century.

The unicorn had achieved a place in legend, religion, and medicine. But it did not stop there.

The unicorn pranced its way into another aspect of medieval life also.

A Political Animal

In the late 1300s Robert III of Scotland despaired of the disorder and violence that wracked his land. He decided that his country could only achieve peace and prosperity through such purity and strength as that of the unicorn. So he had two unicorns carved above a gateway, one on either side of the royal arms of Scotland. In time the unicorns were incorporated into the royal seal of Scotland.

Two centuries later, when James I became king of both Scotland and England, the Scottish unicorn was combined with the traditional English lion of the British Coat of Arms. Author Nancy Hathaway observes that ''throughout history . . . the lion and the unicorn have been linked, for of all the animals the lion is the most majestic, and the unicorn the purest.''

Together these animals seemed a perfect union, but that was not the case. ''One of the fundamental facts concerning lions and unicorns is that they hate each other by instinct,'' says author Odell Shepard. So it was with the English and the Scots. It wasn't until 1707 that the two countries, Scotland and England, were officially united. Even then many Scots resented England.

In the book *Magical Beasts*, author Ruth Manning-Sanders recalls the following rhyme that ''is said to record the old wars between England and Scotland; and since the lion beats the unicorn, it was surely an Englishman who wrote it.''

The lion and the unicorn
Were fighting for the crown;
The lion beat the unicorn
All round the town.

Manning-Sanders adds that ''the enmity between the two beasts is a very old tradition, even going back as far as 3500 B.C. when a fight between the two animals is pictured on a Chaldean chequer-board. [The Chaldeans were an ancient Babylonian people.] Scholars say that the lion stands for summer, the unicorn for spring; so that year after year the lion triumphs over the unicorn, although the undaunted unicorn forever lives to fight another day.''

The rivalry between these two animals is demonstrated again in the tale of the unicorn chasing the lion. Edmund Spenser, in his epic poem *The Faerie Queene*, tells the ancient story in sixteenth-century English. In simpler language it is the tale of a proud, rebellious unicorn who defies the imperial attitude of the lion. The unicorn chases the lion. Both animals are running at top speed when the lion dashes behind a tree. The unicorn, charging in full force and with head lowered, cannot stop. It rams the tree and its precious horn is stuck fast. The unicorn, thus imprisoned, is at the mercy of the lion, who has a ''bounteous feast.''

Left: This French doorway has unicorns carved with a coat of arms, something like Robert III did in Scotland. Above: The English coat of arms.

The unicorn was lavishly depicted in art. Also, its supposed horn was often turned into an artistic charm. Above: A beautifully carved "unicorn" horn (actually, a narwhal horn). Middle: A carving from Praglia Abbey in Italy. Above right: A "lightning rod" from France.

In spite of the implication in this tale that the unicorn could be outsmarted by a lion, the one-horned creature was considered to be an aristocratic beast worthy of gracing the shields of soldiers and the crests of gentlemen. On objects such as royal seals, shields, and as part of the coat of arms of a country, the animals were depicted in detail and are now regarded as works of art.

So the unicorn entered the world of art, but not only as a political animal.

Alicorn as Art

Since pieces of alicorn were so highly prized, they were often set in rings and other jewelry. Fragments worn on delicate chains around the necks of noble ladies served a double purpose. Besides being beautiful, a piece of unicorn jewelry was an amulet, or charm, protecting the wearer from evil and/or disease.

Goblets made from alicorn were one of the most notable forms of medieval art, and some of these goblets can still be seen today. They are ornately carved and decorated with silver and gold, which increases their already considerable value as antiques. A fine example is a goblet with silver-gilt mountings dating somewhere between 1654 and 1666. The horn is mounted on a silver pedestal and a wide silver band encircles the lip. A lid fits over the goblet, much the way one sees lids on beer steins today. A tiny silver

unicorn rears up on its hind legs atop this elegant cover. A carving of a unicorn head has been worked into the spirals on the horn. The carving evokes a ghostly creature, adding to the sense of mystery that surrounds the goblet. This German goblet is on display at the Metropolitan Museum of Art in New York City.

As a symbol of Jesus Christ, the unicorn had a special place in cathedrals and monasteries. A unicorn appears in the twelfth-century mosaic floor in the Otranto Cathedral in Italy. The mosaic has a rug pattern depicting in one circle Adam and Eve, in other circles Old Testament characters, Alexander the Great, a centaur (half man, half horse), and other symbols. The unicorn is shown with a monk thought to be Friar Panteleone, the maker of the mosaic.

Another example is an altar cloth embroidered with sacred beasts including the unicorn, now in Thun Castle, Switzerland. And a unicorn as the symbol of Christ—and therefore purity—graced the top of the crosier, or staff, of an abbot in St. Boniface Church in Fulda, Germany, in the thirteenth century.

Since some of the creatures in these pieces of religious art were pagan symbols—the centaur, for example—their presence in the cathedrals upset more than one clergyman. St. Bernard, founder and abbot of the monastery of Clairvaux, France, objected strongly to all of these decorations. He asked,

What is the meaning of those absurd monstrosities . . . standing in front of the eyes of studious monks? What are those obscene apes doing

The floor of the cathedral in Siena, Italy, has a stone mosaic with a unicorn as one of the animals portrayed.

St. Bernard objected to the depiction of strange, distracting creatures in church art.

there? . . . Those savage lions? . . . Over there a beast, horse in front and goat behind, and again, a horned beast with a horse's rump. Everywhere is such a rich and amazing profusion of different shapes, that one would sooner learn from the statues than from books, sooner spend the whole day doing that alone rather than contemplate the commandments of God.

Author Rüdiger Robert Beer agrees with St. Bernard that the reasons for all these representations are not clear. Beer says they must be a mixture of ancient traditions, pagan superstition, and curiosity about foreign lands. What is clear, according to Beer, is that the exquisite creature known as the unicorn had become "a useful and potent part of Church language, written and artistic."

When hymns were sung in medieval churches it was not unusual for the writer of the lyrics to have included the unicorn as a symbol. One song taken from a collection called Bergkreyen (mountain songs) includes these lines:

Were this unicorn for us not born,
Then all we sinners'd be forlorn,
Unworthily, then, we take him in,
God help us all into his father's realm.

Here the unicorn certainly stands for Jesus Christ, the Savior of the Christians. The lines may be interpreted as meaning that if Christ (the "unicorn") had not been born, it would be a sad situation for sinners. But those that believe ("take him in") will, with God's help, be taken into heaven (Christ's "father's realm").

Perhaps the best known unicorn art is a group of wall hangings, which, like the goblets, is on display in the Cloisters, a part of the Metropolitan Museum of Art in New York City.

In this picture, the unicorn is the symbol of the Holy Spirit in the Holy Trinity of Father, Son, and Holy Spirit.

The Unicorn Tapestries

It is not known for whom the famous Unicorn Tapestries were woven, but it is generally agreed that they were made in Brussels, Belgium, about 1500. One theory is that they were woven for the wedding of Anne of Brittany and her husband Louis XII of France in 1499. Another theory is that the tapestries were commissioned by the noble La Rochefoucauld family for their son François and his second wife, Barbe du Bois. A list of possessions of François VI de La Rochefoucauld made when he died in 1680 includes "tapestries representing a hunt of the unicorn in seven pieces." These adorned the bedroom of his townhouse in Paris.

Through the years the tapestries were moved from place to place in Europe until 1922, when John D. Rockefeller saw them and bought the set. He later donated them to the museum in New York City. However, the fifth tapestry was missing. In 1936, fragments of this last tapestry were found in Paris. The group of seven how hangs in the museum on four walls of an intimate room constructed and furnished like one in a medieval chateau.

John D. Rockefeller purchased the famous unicorn tapestries that hang in the Cloisters in New York City.

One step in the very complicated and time-consuming art of tapestry making.

Who planned and designed these intricately woven wall hangings? No one knows. But Margaret B. Freeman, former curator of the Cloisters, says,

Whoever it was who masterminded the themes of the Unicorn Tapestries, he must have been imbued with the lore of the unicorn, with medieval beliefs about other beasts and birds, and with the "language" of trees and flowers. But he appears to have been an inventive person also, for he conceived the idea of integrating the familiar aspects of the unicorn legend with a fully developed representation of a medieval hunt.

This person, or the one who hired him, must also have thought the unicorn to be a worthy subject for such an undertaking—the making of the tapestries was a monumental project! Designers would have drawn the first sketches, and a painter would have executed them on large linen sheets or on strips of paper pasted together. Then there would be the dyers of the fine silk and woolen threads and those who prepared the metallic threads by winding strips of silver or gilded silver around strands of silk, all to be used for creating the designs.

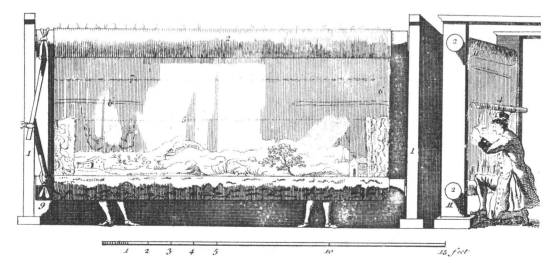

It would have taken many workers to set up the enormous looms with heavy, undyed woolen warp threads, and weavers would have worked countless hours producing in textile form the scenes painted by the artist on linen or paper.

This was an expensive project, one that only the very wealthy could afford. And the subject is no ordinary hunt, but a royal one.

The tapestries portray a medieval stag hunt, only instead of a deer, the hunters are setting forth to capture the legendary unicorn.

The First Tapestry: The Start of the Hunt   In the first tapestry three noblemen are about to begin their search for the unicorn. Their elaborate costumes add

"The unconscious sends all sorts of vapors, odd beings, terrors and deluding images up into the mind—whether in dream, broad daylight, or insanity."

Joseph Campbell in *The Hero with a Thousand Faces*

"Reality is not only stranger than we conceive, but stranger than we can conceive."

Biologist J.S. Haldane

A tapestry from the famous Cluny series in France. These are as beautifully worked as the ones in New York's Cloisters museum. Shown here is the classic scene of the unicorn and the maiden.

The first two tapestries in the Cloisters series: Left, *The Start of the Hunt*. Right, *The Unicorn at the Fountain*.

to the richness and color of the tapestry. Other members of the hunting party are a young *seigneur* or lord, his two companions and the hound keepers who hold their dogs on leashes, waiting for the chase to begin. As on all the tapestries, an abundance of trees, flowers, and shrubbery creates a fantasy setting. By ignoring the seasons, the hangings depict the best of what nature has to offer. For example, a cherry tree laden with midsummer fruit grows beside some springtime daffodils.

The Second Tapestry: The Unicorn at the Fountain Here the huntsmen have surrounded their quarry in a clearing near a castle. But they pause to watch in awe as the gorgeous creamy-white creature dips its horn into a stream to purify the water. The rules of the hunt require the party to hold back until the quarry starts to run, for a harrowing chase is the hunter's greatest challenge.

The Third Tapestry: The Unicorn Leaps the Stream
The hunt is well under way in this hanging. The unicorn plunges into the stream in an effort to elude his pursuers.

The Fourth Tapestry: The Unicorn Defends Himself The hunt has reached its peak now as the unicorn violently defends himself. Ctesias, the Greek physician who wrote about the unicorn in 400 B.C., said, "They fight with thrusts of horn; they kick, bite, and strike with wounding force both horses and hunters."

The third Cloisters tapestry: *The Unicorn Leaps the Stream*.

The fourth tapestry: *The Unicorn Defends Himself.*

In this tapestry the unicorn gores a greyhound and almost topples a hunter with a kick from both hind legs.

The huntsmen move in for the kill as if they believe their target is an ordinary stag. It seems they do not know, or have forgotten, that the only way in which a unicorn can be taken is to lure it to its death. For this it is necessary to employ a virgin maid.

The Fifth Tapestry: The Unicorn Is Captured by the Maiden A young woman has been posted in the forest as bait, while the hunters hide behind trees and inside caves. When the unicorn sees the woman alone it approaches cautiously. Then sensing her gentleness,

The fifth and sixth tapestries: Left, *The Unicorn Is Captured by the Maiden*. Right, *The Unicorn Is Killed and Brought to the Castle*.

it comes to rest beside her with its head in her lap. While the unicorn gazes adoringly at the young woman, the hunters steal up and—the unicorn is taken. (The idea that a unicorn could only be captured by a maiden is so old no one knows where or how it began, but it precedes the Unicorn Tapestries.)

In the fragments of the fifth tapestry a second woman seems to be signalling the hunters that the unicorn has been subdued. Only the fingers of the innocent maiden can be seen caressing the unicorn's mane.

The Sixth Tapestry: The Unicorn Is Killed and Brought to the Castle Two important episodes of the unicorn legend occur here. At the upper left the dogs are attacking the hapless creature, and spears pierce its flesh. The hunter blowing his horn forms a transition between the bloody killing and the delivering of the unicorn to the castle gate where the lord and lady wait to receive it.

The seventh, and perhaps the most famous, Cloisters tapestry: *The Unicorn in Captivity*.

The Seventh Tapestry: The Unicorn in Captivity
In the last tapestry the unicorn has miraculously come to life again and rests within a circular wooden enclosure. Here the unicorn is interpreted by many people to be the risen Christ in the midst of a paradisiac garden.

Another explanation is given by Linda Sipress in a study of the Unicorn Tapestries. She says, "This scene [the Unicorn in Captivity] is not related in any way to the medieval stag hunt, but is the finale to the allegorical love hunt described by medieval poets and writers." Since the unicorn is shown collared and chained to a tree he is the image of the lover-bridegroom, at last secured by his adored lady, his bride.

No doubt these famous tapestries did their share in spreading the belief that the unicorn was a real animal as well as a symbolic one.

Peter Lum, in his book *Fabulous Beasts*, says, "The unicorn was in fact the only one of the nonexistent animals described in the Physiologus that survived through the Renaissance [fourteenth through seventeenth centuries], and could still be taken for granted in the eighteenth and nineteenth centuries. Even the most learned naturalists . . . could not quite deny the unicorn."

Letters such as those supposedly written by the mysterious Prester John, beliefs in the curative powers of alicorn, and the use of the unicorn in art and as a Christian symbol all contributed to the lore of the unicorn.

But was it just folklore? Or are there factual bases for beliefs about unicorns?

"It is marvelously clear that when the unicorn was first described and centuries later when the tapestries were woven, everyone believed in unicorns."

Marianna Mayer, *The Unicorn and the Lake*

"It is a creature which never existed but has nonetheless fascinated man for thousands of years."

Rüdiger Robert Beer, *Unicorn: Myth and Reality*

Six

Science and the Unicorn

From time to time attempts have been made to pull the unicorn out of the shadows of art, literature, and religion to examine the creature in the light of scientific thinking. Some people, like Aristotle, try to explain away the magic power, focusing instead on the reasons such a creature is possible. They try to place it on the same level as the camel, the elephant, and the giraffe. Others, like St. Hildegard, conceded that it had mysterious powers, but declared that its ability to heal was due to its superior diet. Alanus de Insulis, a twelfth-century scholar, also tried to apply science to the unicorn. He explained that the unicorn was attracted to an innocent maiden because the animal "has an excess of fervent spirits or humours [hot fluids] which dilate his heart, and when it comes into the pure moist air surrounding the virgin he feels such relief and is so delighted by that feminine atmosphere that he lies down in her lap."

In medieval times a humor was one of four fluids in the body thought to determine a person's health and temperament. Alanus de Insulis did the best he could with the knowledge available to him. And who was there to say he wasn't correct?

Centuries later other scientists were still trying to probe the mysteries of the unicorn. Later efforts were

A modern-day unicorn. Lancelot, developed by a California couple, traveled around the country to medieval-style fairs.

"It was science which finally deposed the unicorn—and it was science which resurrected it."

Nancy Hathaway, *The Unicorn*

"Eventually scientific observation (or lack of it) won out, and the animal was declared a figment of the imagination."

Anthony S. Mercante, *Zoo of the Gods*

directed toward discovering whether unicorns really did exist—in the past or in the present. They needed concrete evidence. Fossils provided a possible clue.

Digging Up the Bones

In 1663 some bones were unearthed in a limestone cave near Quedlinburg, north of the Harz Mountains in Germany. According to author Rüdiger Robert Beer, "People flocked to the excavation and many pocketed a few bones as souvenirs; bones there were to spare, for the cave was full of fossil remains." Finally the abbess of Quedlinburg was able to restore order. The excavations proceeded methodically and the famous scientist Otto von Guericke undertook to reconstruct a skeleton from the debris. Von Guericke's name is known to this day for his experiments with vacuums and atmospheric pressure, but he was also an investigator in the field of natural science.

Reconstruction of the Quedlinburg unicorn. Most likely the skeleton was put together incorrectly.

The skeleton von Guericke pieced together had only two legs and seemed to rely for support on its powerful tail. But its most astounding feature was its single horn, seven and one-half feet in length—longer than a man is tall. The horn protruded majestically from the center of the creature's large head. Von Guericke's reconstruction caused a sensation!

Perhaps some of the people gathered around that limestone cave had read what the Roman, Julius Caesar, had written about an animal living in the Hercynian Forest of Germany. This statesman, soldier, and author invaded Germany between 60 and 55 B.C. In the *Gallic Wars*, Caesar wrote:

> It is known that many kinds of animals not seen in other places breed therein. . . . There is an ox, shaped like a stag [deer], from the middle of whose forehead, between the ears, stands forth a single horn, taller and straighter than the horns we know.

Did this mean that the fossil remains were those of a beast that was the forerunner of the one-horned creature Caesar described? Did a form of unicorn inhabit Europe at the time of the dinosaurs?

Additional weight was given to this possibility by Baron Gottfried Wilhelm von Leibniz (1646-1716), a German philosopher, mathematician, and scientist. Leibniz included a drawing of von Guericke's reconstructed unicorn in the *Protogaea*, a history of this area of Germany and the life it contained in the distant past.

Although author Odell Shepard reports that Leibniz formerly had some doubts as to the existence of the unicorn, the Quedlinburg skeleton and a similar one found in the nearby mountains at Scharzfeld "converted him entirely."

The German fossils were not the only ones that supported the theory that unicorns once roamed the earth. Beer writes about some found in the U.S.S.R.:

> A few skeletal fragments found in Russia and Siberia belong to an animal which has been given

Julius Caesar recorded that unicorn-like creatures inhabited German forests.

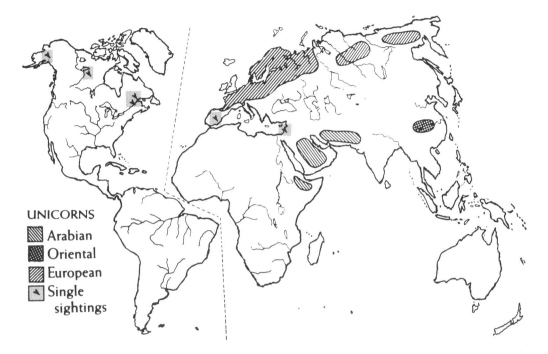

Map of unicorn territory, showing the places unicorns have been sighted over the centuries. From Paul and Karin Johnsgard's fanciful book, *Dragons and Unicorns: A Natural History*.

the scientific name of Elasmotherium (literally "armor-plated beast"). It was the size of an elephant but rather closer to the rhinoceros in physique, although its nasal region was too weak to have supported a horn. Nevertheless, skulls which have been discovered show an extraordinarily thick osseous [bony] pad on the forehead, which was clearly intended to support an immense horn.

It is within reason that this animal might have been exterminated by its human neighbors in Siberia. There are reports that the elasmotherium has been found on rare occasions in the Rhineland [Germany], although we have no knowledge of any museum where such remains may have been preserved. Had our primitive ancestors actually seen such a monster, it might indeed have been the source of a primeval conception of the unicorn!

The bones found in Germany and Siberia were flimsy evidence, to some people's way of thinking. Author Odell Shepard believes the German fossil unicorn bones, and scores of others were probably not bones at all but stalactites and stalagmites frequently found in caves. These formations are made when water drips from the ceiling of the dank cavern. They resemble icicles—or a horn. Shepard says other so-called bones were petrified wood. But he has no evidence to support his opinion. Wouldn't scientists such as Otto von Guericke and Baron von Leibniz have known the difference between stalactite formations, wood, and bones?

Were the skeletons real?

Did some of these creatures escape extinction to live on in hidden places? People in the seventeenth century were not sure. Those who wanted to believe could only hope that somewhere on high mountains or in deep valleys unicorns still lived.

Even this hope was seemingly shattered by an announcement in 1827 by a French naturalist, Baron Georges Leopold Cuvier.

Baron Cuvier was a respected scientist who had done a great deal of research in the field of ancient animals. Cuvier said that unicorns did not exist—and

Do unicorns still live in hidden places? Early twentieth-century artist Arthur Davies seems to think so.

Do unicorns have cloven hoofs like a deer (left) or solid hoofs like a horse (right)? Artists and writers through the ages have disagreed about this.

never had. He based his opinion on the idea that unicorns had cloven hoofs.

Long before Cuvier's time it was believed that unicorns had solid hoofs, like those of a horse. This was the basis of Aristotle's theory that because a solid hoof requires more horny substance, there is only enough left over to produce one horn.

But throughout the Middle Ages, medieval art showed the unicorn with *cloven* hoofs. Therefore, Cuvier said, it was impossible for the unicorn to have a single horn. An animal with divided hoofs would have a frontal bone on the forehead that would be divided also. It would have *two* horns, or none at all. No single horn, said Cuvier, could grow above the division.

Unicorns in the Zoo

Maybe Cuvier was right. Maybe no single horn grew *naturally* from two frontal lobes on the skull. But unicorns had been *seen*. In 1906 two unicorn rams [male sheep] were on display at the zoo in London, England. These animals had been presented to the Prince of Wales as part of a large collection of animals from the country of Nepal in Asia. Author Peter Costello says: "There was some mystery about the creatures, for though the rams were unicorns, underneath the horn sheath were found two horn buds.

Further inquiries revealed that they were not natural, nor were they freaks, but artificial creations.''

Artificial Unicorns

That a unicorn could be produced artificially had been suggested a number of times in the past. In 1796, a French traveler, known as LeVaillant, described a process of manipulating the horns of oxen. In his *Travels in Africa*, he wrote:

> As the horns of the young ox sprout they are trained over the forehead until the points meet. They are then manipulated so as to make them coalesce [grow together], and so shoot upwards from the middle of the forehead, like the horn of the fabled unicorn.

Many centuries before LeVaillant, the Roman called Pliny the Elder had written about a method of twisting horns together. ''And in very truth the hornes of these beasts [oxen] are of so pliable a substance . . . that as they grow upon their heads, even whilst the beasts are living, they may with boiling wax be bended and turned every way as a man will.''

Another process of creating a unicorn out of an ordinary animal was reported by W.S. Berridge in *Marvels of the Animal World*, in 1921.

> By certain maltreatment ordinary two-horned sheep are converted into a one-horned variety. The process adopted is branding with a red-hot iron the male lambs when about two or three months old on their horns when they are beginning to sprout. The wounds are treated with a mixture of oil and soot and when they heal, instead of growing at their usual places and spreading, come out as one from the middle of the skull.

Since Berridge was the British Resident at the Court of Nepal, it seemed as if this explained how the unicorn rams in the London Zoo had been created. But Berridge was doubtful that this was so. He goes on to say:

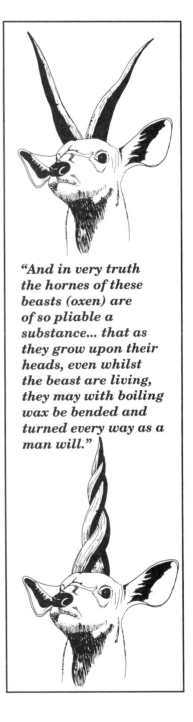

"And in very truth the hornes of these beasts (oxen) are of so pliable a substance... that as they grow upon their heads, even whilst the beast are living, they may with boiling wax be bended and turned every way as a man will."

African Kaffirs manipulating cattle horns.

Notwithstanding the above explanation, the majority of naturalists are inclined to doubt whether a true understanding has yet been arrived at concerning these sheep [of Nepal], for it has been pointed out that the mere fact of searing the budding horns would not result in those appendages sprouting out at the summit of the skull instead of towards the side, and moreover, if there is any secret attending their production it has been remarkably well kept from the ever-prying eyes of zoologists. It is true that the horns of a young animal might be induced to grow together by binding them up, but in that case we should expect the bony supports to be bent aside at their bases as a result of the unnatural strain put upon them, whereas on the contrary, those of the unicorn sheep arise in quite a straight manner from the skull.

Though scientists generally agree that the unicorns given to the English royalty in 1906 must have been artificially made, the process remains shrouded in mystery.

According to Peter Costello, author of *The Magic Zoo*, artificial unicorns were created in Africa, also. This was done by tribes along the White Nile River in northern Africa and by the Nandi tribe in Kenya.

Do these reports of artificial unicorns explain the one-horned cows and bulls that Aelianus says were to be found in Ethiopia around A.D. 200?

Dr. W. Franklin Dove, an American biologist, decided to find out.

Dr. Dove's Experiment

In an article in *Scientific Monthly* magazine, May 1936, Dr. Dove discussed an experiment carried out an the University of Maine.

Dr. Dove says Cuvier was mistaken in his idea of horn structure. Horns "are not outgrowths of the skull bones" but are formed separately and then rooted to the skull; they do not emerge from it. Therefore, these separate horn buds (small bits of tissue that later produce horn) can be transplanted in whole or in part to other regions of the head where they take root. "They develop as true horns . . . either solidly or loosely attached to the skull, according to the method of transplantation."

In March 1933, an operation was performed on a day-old Ayrshire calf. Two horn buds were trans-

Left: Calf's skull, on which the two horn buds have been moved together. Right: Dr. Dove's fifteen-month-old unicorn-calf. The two horn buds fused together, making a single, solid horn.

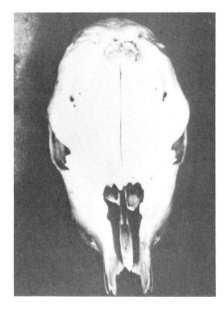

> "The horn of the
> unicorn . . . remains even
> to the present time, a
> mystery."
>
> Dr. W. Franklin Dove, developer of
> a unicorn-calf

> "The horn between its eyes
> is also its all-penetrating
> spirit."
>
> Ernst Fuchs, painter and illustrator

planted to the center of the calf's skull so that they lay side by side over the frontal division of the skull. Since the horn buds are normally round, Dove trimmed them so that they were flat along the sides where they touched. Thus they made closer contact. "It was expected that the two horns would fuse together into one large horn solidly attached to the skull and located between and somewhat above the eyes, as is the horn of the unicorn."

The experiment was successful!

At two and a half years old, Dr. Dove reported, this cow used its single horn "as a prow to pass under fences and barriers in his path, or as a forward thrusting bayonet in his attacks." While a two-horned animal must make side cuts and slashes, the unicorn can put its full body weight behind its one horn. It becomes almost invincible.

Moreover, the unicorn is conscious of its unusual power. This consciousness, claims Dr. Dove, makes the creature docile, a characteristic found also in the legendary one-horned beast.

Did people in the Middle Ages keep pet unicorns, or is this merely a fanciful painting?

Using a reference in Latin from Pliny as his source, Dr. Dove asserts that the early Romans had the secret of horn-bud transplantation, too. But why was this done? It may have been to distinguish the leader from the rest of the herd. Dr. Dove believed, as the result of his experiment, that a creature not necessarily born to be a leader, *becomes* one when it develops a single horn. He wrote:

> We can not say that the ancients made unicorns of the leaders of their herds, especially in view of the fact that such a transplantation as we have described must be effected shortly after birth when qualities of leadership are not yet discernible. But we say rather that the presence of a single horn upon the forehead of any single beast in the herd or flock gave it the incentive for leadership through a power which it learned only by experience.

Dr. Dove's unicorn calf certainly did not have the mystery and grace that was associated with the European unicorn. But his experiment shed some light on a possible explanation for the Chinese Ki-Lin, which

There were many questions Dr. Dove's experiment left unanswered. None of the unicorns popularly pictured throughout history resembled a cow. Could a horse-unicorn or a goat-unicorn be as easily created?

had been described by some as the size and shape of a calf.

Dr. Dove, in making a case for his theory of artificial unicorns, says it may be that Ctesias's unicorn of 400 B.C. did not actually have a red-tipped horn as reported. It may have been that the light reflected from the black tip made it appear scarlet. This is not an uncommon occurrence, according to the doctor. He also points out that if he had used a female Ayrshire calf rather than a male, the tip of the horn would have been red, for the color difference is a sex-linked genetic trait in this breed.

Ctesias's description then of a three-colored horn is not as far-fetched as it might have at first seemed. But how does Dr. Dove account for the wild ass's horse-like shape? And if these were artificially made unicorns, why were they running wild?

Dr. Dove's experiment left some questions still unanswered.

For almost fifty years, it seemed the mystery of the origin of unicorns would be forever lost in the mists of time. Perhaps no one cared anymore.

Then in 1980, pictures of a ''living unicorn'' hit the United States newspapers. To skeptics the animal looked like a goat. But it was no ordinary goat. From the middle of its forehead there did indeed grow a ten-inch horn!

Born in California

This goat-like creature, alive today, is an appealing animal, bred of Angora goat stock, so its coat is white and soft. Its name is Lancelot.

Lancelot's creators are two naturalists, Morning Glory and her husband Otter G'Zell, who do not hide the fact that they created Lancelot and that its mother was a goat. They describe their unicorn in terms more poetic than scientific:

Lancelot is a true medieval-type Unicorn: a silken snowy wonder with flowing mane, bearded chin, and

Opposite page: Lancelot, the living goat-unicorn, bred by Morning Glory and Otter G'Zell.

plumed tail, who walks the Earth on dainty cloven hooves, a golden horn growing from the center of his brow. As in the legends, he can be gentle or fierce; he has penetrating powers of discernment and a fondness for young maidens.

Since the birth of Lancelot, these naturalists have bred other single-horned animals which resemble the unicorns on the medieval tapestries. Morning Glory and G'Zell do not go into detail about their methods of achieving one horn on an animal that would ordinarily have two. Nor do they describe the technique they claim to have pioneered for taking away the "obnoxious billy goat stink" that they say contributes to some undesirable behaviors. They do admit to having clipped the unicorn's hair to produce a flowing mane, plumed tail, and feathers of hair on the legs. In addition they have "conducted appropriate magickal rites, invoking the spirits of Nature and the Horned God, and focusing the light of the waxing Moon onto their [the unicorns'] foreheads through a quartz crystal." All these devices, "and others more subtle, go into the production of a true Unicorn," according to Morning Glory and G'Zell.

Lancelot in the Circus

They believe so strongly that what they have created is something special that they want to share their unicorns with the world. "A live unicorn could be an international ambassador of good will," they say, "since the Unicorn is a cross-cultural symbol. Lancelot is also the ultimate symbol for endangered species that have made a comeback."

Controversy and outrage developed when Lancelot was put on display with Ringling Brothers and Barnum and Bailey Circus in 1980. John Kullberg, then president of the American Society for the Prevention of Cruelty to Animals, called Lancelot a goat which had been subjected to an inhumane implant of a bull's horn.

But what of the other characteristics attributed to unicorns? In a booklet called *The Living Unicorn* put out by a group in California, the un-named author explains that, ''The single horn growing from the center of his forehead is located above the pineal gland, or 'third eye,' the master gland that ultimately governs the function of the endocrine glands such as the pituitary and, so the mystics say, the psychic centers of the brain. Therefore, the Unicorn may grow to be larger, more intelligent and more sensitive than other animals of his ancestral stock.''

Does this mean that having a horn growing directly above a gland is what makes a unicorn stronger, yet more gentle than others of its kind? Or is Dr. Dove right when he says that having one horn simply causes an animal to become a leader? If unicorns were bred, or medically altered, to be leaders of herds, how did they gain the reputation of being solitary creatures?

And what of the powers that the ancient unicorns were said to have—the power to remove poison from a stream, to cure dreaded diseases, and to ward off evil? Artificial unicorns have none of these powers.

Morning Glory and G'Zell, Dr. Dove, and the people in Africa and Nepal all created one-horned animals. But are the creatures they created just synthetic versions of the most superior animal of them all?

A medieval coin depicting a goat-like unicorn.

Epilogue

Where Are the Unicorns Now?

Some people would say that unicorns are no more, that they are extinct. Others would say they never were, that they lived only in myth or in the minds of those who wanted to believe. Some say one-horned creatures are seen only in dreams.

Author Anthony Shepherd believes so strongly that antelopes were mistaken for unicorns, that he would say unicorns can be found today in the Phoenix Zoo in Arizona, where a herd of Arabian oryx lives in captivity.

Caroline Feller Bauer in an article in *Cricket* magazine says, "You can search the woods and fields and even the city streets, but the easiest way to meet a unicorn is in books." She may be right. But who knows which stories are based on fact, and which are fiction?

Who knows what made Genghis Khan turn back from conquering India? Or why peasants and kings alike thought alicorn powder cured their ills and kept them from being poisoned? And who can say, when the scent of cinnamon lingers in the air, that a unicorn has not just passed by? Who really knows?

All that is certain is that unicorns have galloped through history, leaving behind them a trail of questions.

Will they ever be answered?

Appendix

The Unicorn Today

Author Daniel Cohen in *The Encyclopedia of Monsters* says, "Today we are in the midst of what must be called a unicorn revival. We find the symbol of the unicorn on everything from stationery to sheets—it is more popular than it has ever been." Why is this true? Does anyone still believe in the power of the horn?

Author Odell Shepard notes that "there has existed from early times and in many parts of the world a vague notion that horns in general, almost any kind of horns, are somehow prophylactic [preventing of disease]." As an example, Shepard says, "I have myself encountered in western America the idea that nothing drunk from a cow's horn can ever harm the drinker."

Cohen goes on to say, "Even today, rhinoceros horn is regarded as both a universal remedy and powerful aphrodisiac [something that excites sexual desire] throughout much of the Middle East." And in 1981, an article in the Minneapolis *Tribune* told of the concern in Kenya, Uganda, and northern Tanzania that if rhinoceroses continued to be killed at the rate they were in 1970, there would not be "a single rhino left in the East African wild by 1990." At that time in the Arab state of North Yemen, young men paid up to $13,000 for a dagger with a carved handle of rhino horn.

Stories such as this reinforce the theory that unicorns may have become extinct for the same reasons that the rhino is now an endangered species.

**Tests for True
Unicorn Horn**

Draw a ring on the floor
with the alicorn. Place a
spider in the ring. If it
cannot cross the line, but
stays trapped inside until
it starves to death, the
horn is real.

Lay the horn near a
poisonous plant or animal.
If the horn is true alicorn
the plant or animal will
burst and die.

Plunge the horn in water.
If the water bubbles and
appears to boil—but in
fact remains cold—this
is true alicorn.

Place a piece of silk upon
a burning coal, then lay the
horn on top of the silk.
If the horn came from a
unicorn, and not from a
goat or bull or sheep, the
silk will not be burned.

Is there any basis for believing that horn was—or
is—an effective cure? There may have been. Another
common medieval practice—that of blood letting—
used leeches [bloodsucking worms] in attempts to cure
patients. While this may sound far-fetched, Israeli
scientists, in 1988, reported discovering two enzymes
in leech saliva that help keep blood from clotting and
that may be used to fight blood disorders. If unicorn
horn—or its liver or fat or hoofs—were tested today,
would similar uses be found for it?

Even if this were possible, and no medicinal value
were found for alicorn, author Nancy Hathaway
believes the beautiful creature still would have enormous appeal in the modern world. She says it is easy
to see why:

> In a world suffering from pollution, the unicorn
> can purify water with a single dip of its horn. In
> a world where animals are becoming extinct, the
> unicorn can never die. In a world where we might
> literally blow ourselves up at any moment, the
> unicorn harkens back to another time and a better
> life. The unicorn symbolizes sensitivity coupled
> with strength, the lure of sexuality and nature
> linked with the power of purity and truth. Today,
> when it is difficult to believe in these things any
> longer, the unicorn reminds us of a time when good
> existed—when unicorns existed. In a time when
> the future is looking bleak, the unicorn is a sym-
> bol not just of hope but of strength; it tells us that
> the unattainable is worth striving for, worth
> searching for, worth believing in—even if it ex-
> ists only in our minds.

Bruce Coville, who compiled and edited *The
Unicorn Treasury*, agrees. He says, "Here's what I
believe: wherever else they may have come from,
unicorns live inside the true believer's heart.

"Which means that as long as we can dream, there
will be unicorns."

For Further Exploration

Rüdiger Robert Beer, *Unicorn: Myth and Reality.* New York: Van Nostrand Reinhold Co., 1972.

Daniel Cohen, *The Encyclopedia of Monsters.* New York: Dodd, Mead and Co., 1982.

Peter Costello, *The Magic Zoo: The Natural History of Fabulous Animals.* New York: St. Martin's Press, 1979.

Bruce Coville, *The Unicorn Treasury.* New York: Doubleday, 1988.

Margaret B. Freeman, *The Unicorn Tapestries.* New York: The Metropolitan Museum of Art, 1976.

Nancy Hathaway, *The Unicorn.* New York: Viking Press, 1980.

Peter Lum, *Fabulous Beasts.* New York: Pantheon, 1951.

Odell Shepard, *The Lore of the Unicorn.* New York: Harper and Row, 1930.

Anthony Shepherd, *The Flight of the Unicorns.* New York: Abelard-Schuman, 1965.

PERIODICALS

Caroline Feller Bauer, "Unicorns Do Exist." *Cricket.* 15:38; May, 1988.

FICTION

Peter S. Beagle, *The Last Unicorn.* New York: Viking Press, 1968.

Barbara Cohen, *Unicorns in the Rain.* New York: Atheneum, 1980.

Madeleine L'Engle, *A Swiftly Tilting Planet.* New York: Farrar, Straus and Giroux, Inc., 1987.

C.S. Lewis, *The Last Battle.* (Seventh in the Chronicles of Narnia). New York: Macmillan, 1956.

Additional Bibliography

Sabine Baring-Gould, *Curious Myths of the Middle Ages*. London: Longmans, Green and Co., 1906.

Jorge Luis Borges, with Margarita Guerrero, *The Book of Imaginary Beings*. New York: E.P. Dutton and Co., Inc., 1969.

T.J. Elliott, *A Medieval Bestiary*. (Translated and introduced by T.J. Elliott.) Boston: Godine, 1971.

Ernst and Johanna Lehner, *A Fantastic Bestiary*. New York: Tudor Publishing Co., 1969.

The Living Unicorn, no author given, P.O. Box 369, Los Gatos, CA 95031.

Ruth Manning-Sanders, *Magical Beasts*. New York: Thomas Nelson, Inc., 1970.

Anthony S. Mercante, *Zoo of the Gods*. New York: Harper and Row, 1974.

Edward Topsell, *The Elizabethan Zoo: A Book of Beasts Both Fabulous and Authentic*. Boston: David R. Godine, 1979.

T.H. White, *The Bestiary: A Book of Beasts*. New York: G.P. Putnam's Sons, 1953.

PERIODICALS

Dr. W. Franklin Dove, "Artificial Production of the Fabulous Unicorn: A Modern Interpretation of an Ancient Myth." *The Scientific Monthly*. 42:431-436; May, 1936.

Noel D. Vietmeyer, "Rare Narwhal Inspired the Myth of the Unicorn," *Smithsonian*. 10:118-123; Feb., 1980.

FICTION

Margaret Greaves, *A Net to Catch the Wind*. New York: Harper and Row, Inc., 1979.

Nancy Luenn, *Unicorn Crossing*. New York, Atheneum, 1987.

Marianna Mayer, *The Unicorn and the Lake*. New York: The Dial Press, 1982.

Index

Aelian, 40-41
Alexander III, 56-57
alicorn, 61, 63-65, 72, 102
Apollonius, 41
Aristotle, 36, 38, 90

Baring-Gould, Sabine, 56, 59
Bauer, Caroline Feller, 102
Beer, Rüdiger Robert, 16, 19, 38, 51, 61, 74, 86, 87-88
Berridge, W.S., 91-92
Borges, Jorge Luis, 22, 24, 25

Caesar, Julius, 87
Carruthers, Douglas, 34
Ching-tsae, 26-27
Cohen, Daniel, 15
Confucius, 26, 27-28, 30
Costello, Peter, 90-91, 92
Ctesias, 14-16, 17, 18, 36, 38, 41, 57, 60, 79, 96
Cuvier, Georges Leopold, 89-90, 93

Daniel, 44-45, 47
de Insulis, Alanus, 84
Dove, W. Franklin, 93-96, 101

Freeman, Margaret B., 75-76
Frobisher, Martin, 68-69

Gesner, Conrad, 64-65
G'Zell, Morning Glory and Otter, 96, 98, 101

Hathaway, Nancy, 18, 25, 26, 45, 48, 54, 70

Jenner, Edward, 66
John, Prester (Presbyter Johannes), 56-60, 83
John of Hesse, 60

Khan, Genghis, 10-13, 14, 15, 16, 17, 27, 102

Lancelot the unicorn, 96, 98, 101
La Rochefoucauld family, 75-76
Leibniz, Gottfried Wilhelm von, 87, 89

Manning-Sanders, Ruth, 70-71
Megasthenes, 38-39

Noah, 51-52

Otranto Cathedral (Italy), 73

Paré, Ambroise, 67
Physiologus, 48-49
Pliny the elder (Gaius Plinius Secundus), 39-40, 41, 91
Polo, Marco, 59-60

Quedlinburg (Germany), 86, 87

Robert II of Scotland, 70
Rockefeller, John D., 75

St. Ambrose, 50-51
St. Bernard, 73-74
St. Hildegard, 63-64, 84
sea-unicorns, 68
Shepard, Odell, 12, 20, 23, 25, 28, 39, 40, 44, 66, 70, 87, 88-89
Shepherd, Anthony, 30, 33, 102
Sipress, Linda, 81-82
Spenser, Edmund, 71
Ssetsen, Ssanang, 12

Toms, Gerald, 99

unicorns
  and the biblical flood, 51-52
  and virgins, 80, 84
  as artificial, 91-101

as extinct, 18, 86-89
as mutants, 18-19
as supernatural, 16, 25-26, 28, 30-35
belief in,
  ancient, 10-53
  Arabian, 30-35, 38, 54
  Buddhist, 14
  Chinese, 22-28, 30, 95
  European, 40-41, 42-83
  Indian, 12-13, 14, 36, 38-39
  Japanese, 28-30
  medieval, 54-83
  modern, 96-101
  origins of, 14-18
bones of, 86-89
  ankle-bone, 40-41
capture of, 36, 40
food of, 66
forms of,
  cartazoon, 38-39
  karkadann, 30, 32
  Ki-Lin, 20-28, 95
  kirin, 28-30
hoofs of, 36, 38, 90
horns of, 15, 17-18, 22, 28, 29, 30, 32, 33,
  38, 40, 50, 65-66, 69, 71, 87, 96
  as spiral, 18, 39, 54, 69
  testing of, 61, 63, 65, 69
  value of, 67, 69-70
in art, 72-83
in Christianity, 42, 44-52, 72-75
in zoos, 90-91, 102
legends of, 14-18, 20-23, 26-35
lifespan of, 23
linked to lion, 70-71
powers of,
  discerning right and wrong, 29-30
  ensuring safety, 72
  healing, 32-33, 35, 38, 41, 60-61, 63-67
qualities of,
  ability to predict future, 16, 25-26, 28, 30,
    45, 47
  cinnamon scent of, 18, 26, 102
  ferociousness, 28-30, 44, 79
  gentleness, 39, 94, 101
  purity, 50, 70, 73

strength, 44, 50, 66, 70, 101
resembling,
  antelope, 32, 33, 44
  asses, 14-15, 36, 38, 41, 96
  bulls, 17, 28
  deer, 29, 40, 87
  gazelle, 14
  goats, 17, 29, 45, 49, 96, 98-99
  horses, 15, 17, 20, 38, 40
  mountain sheep, 14
  narwhal, 68-70
  oryx, 33-35, 44
  oxen, 44, 87
  rhinoceros, 15, 39, 44, 88
unicorn tapestries, 75-83
  creation of, 76-77
  themes of, 76, 77-82

Vietmeyer, Noel D., 68-69
von Guericke, Otto, 86-89

Webbe, Edward, 59

Picture Credits

About the Author

Norma Gaffron, a former school teacher, lives in New Brighton, Minnesota.

Norma has been writing professionally for the past eleven years. Her articles, on topics as diverse as sailing, snakes, and replanting lost teeth, have appeared in many national magazines. She has been a Junior Great Books leader and is regional advisor for the National Society of Children's Book Writers. She and her husband have three grown children.

Norma likes to write and to explore ideas that hover on the fringe of reality. She says, "I continue to look for unicorns. The best time, I've heard, is in those misty moments when darkness turns to dawn. Then, if you're lucky, you may catch a glimpse of one whirling away through the trees. And if you hear its voice it will be as clear as the ringing of a monastery bell."

Unicorns: Opposing Viewpoints is Norma's third book in the Great Mysteries series.